GLOBAL POVERTY AND PERSONAL RESPONSIBILITY

Integrity Through Commitment

by
Elizabeth Morgan

with
Van Weigel,
Research Consultant

and
Eric DeBaufre,
Research Assistant

PAULIST PRESS
New York/Mahwah

Library of Congress Cataloging-in-Publication Data

Morgan, Elizabeth, 1943–
    Global poverty and personal responsibility : integrity through commitment / by Elizabeth Morgan, with Van Weigel and Eric DeBaufre.
      p. cm.
   ISBN 0-8091-3097-1
   1. Economic assistance—Developing countries—Moral and ethical aspects. 2. Basic needs—Developing countries—Moral and ethical aspects. 3. Poverty—Moral and ethical aspects. I. Weigel, Van B., 1954–   . II. DeBaufre, Eric. III. Title.
HC60.M648 1989
338.9′009172′4—dc20   89-35410
                                                     CIP

Published by Paulist Press
997 Macarthur Boulevard
Mahwah, NJ 07430

Printed and bound in the
United States of America

Contents

PART III
A REALISTIC LOOK AT STRATEGIES
FOR SUSTAINED RESPONSE

for JENNY
whose quiet integrity
proves the point

*and with thanks to Denis Goulet of the University of Notre Dame
and Lawrence Pezzullo of Catholic Relief Services
for their interest and assistance*

Preface

A free person is a whole person. A whole person cares about the freedom and potential for wholeness of others. This connection between personal and global integrity forms the very basis of this book.

The design of the book is circular. It moves from the moral self, through a world crying with needs, and back to the question of what one person/one community can do. Yet we hope that the tension between personal and global integrity is present *throughout* the chapters and that it infuses energy into every discussion. The instigation of thoughtful, praxis-oriented discussion is what this volume is all about.

Part I examines various bases of individual moral behavior. It looks at justice for the poor as a cross-cultural ethical mandate and encourages the reader/discussant to become self-reflective about his or her method of making ethical decisions. Part II moves from the psychic microcosm to the experiential macrocosm. It examines the empirical reality of world poverty, working with such questions as: What does absolute poverty look like? What are its causes? Part III outlines strategies for combatting absolute poverty—moving from the macrocosm (world community) back to the microcosm (individual and small group action).

You can read this book alone, but we urge you to read it with someone. Each chapter provides the basis for a study session. Members of a study group should covenant to read the textual material, to ponder discussion questions/exercises supplied at the end of each chapter, *and* to add concerns of their own. One way of doing this is to keep response journals—notebooks where reactions can be recorded *as one reads*. (There is tremendous value in getting a reaction into words before it "evaporates" and gives way to the opinions of the strongest personality of one's interpretive community.)

These ten sessions can be used in church school classes, university study groups, community organizations, or among friends. If your group meets at night, you might consider beginning with a pot-luck supper and time of general sharing, before doing the necessary and strenuous work of world-*study* and world-*shaping*.

Studying and shaping should be connected for you, no less than self and world, for knowledge without action is effete, and action without thought is often exhibitionist and bumbling. We suggest that you adopt at least one economic development project during the duration of your work with this book, and that at the end you map out a plan of further study and of increased action.

Toward the continuation of your study, we supply a bibliography at the end of each chapter. Choose an area of interest and explore it, whether it be a particular third world country, the problem of lifestyle, or political action. Toward increased action, any of the agencies listed in Chapter Seven, with addresses, can help you get started. If you are a church/synagogue group, your own denomination will have suggestions for active involvement.

The goal of ending absolute poverty seems overwhelming. It will take massive education and structural change. Until such change can occur *and* as a means of bringing it about, make your study community a *model* of responsible behavior. Learn all that you can; it is the incomprehensible, not the complex that paralyzes human will. Reach out to the extent that you are able; helping to liberate others from the bondage of poverty will liberate you from addictive materialism. Hold your neighbor and yourself with equal respect; justice emerges from such mutuality.

A Note on Naming

Talking about tensions and cooperation between the "haves" and the "have-nots" of the world is tricky business because most of our ways of naming the participants suggest that the "goal" lies with the haves and/or describe static categories. The first world/third world designation is one we are all familiar with, but "first" suggests a "winner," and that association doesn't fit a scheme of things where the poor have so much to teach the rich about endurance and human dignity.

One can speak of rich nations and poor nations, but that limits the discussion to money, as does the hierarchy of high-income, middle-income, and low-income countries. To speak of nations at the center and of those on the periphery describes economic realities, but also suggests "centeredness" vs. "fragmentation" which, when applied to lifestyle, may well reverse the designations.

To speak of the west as over against new nations gets into history (colonialism) but is geographically inaccurate. In terms of hemisphere, north/south makes more sense, since most industrialized nations are above the equator and many new nations are below. But that leads one suspiciously close to the issue of racial/genetic differentiations. Developed vs. developing nations raises the hackles of liberationists reacting against development economics of the 1950's and, again, presents "developed" as an end point—the goal. But this pair of words does have the advantage of suggesting more than economic growth (the evolution of institutions and human well-being as well) and connotes process in that it alone plays on a verb.

In this study, we use all designations from time to time, recognizing their limitations and waiting for a time when economic nomenclature allows more fully for sociological and ethical reasoning.

3

PART I

A REALISTIC LOOK
AT MORAL RESPONSIBILITY

1

Moral Development and Globalization

Chapter One deals with how human beings arrive at the values that govern their behavior. It also explores the way that global moral action can become a vehicle for personal moral "growth." Chapter Two discusses systems of values (Judaism, Christianity, Marxism, and capitalism), illustrating that they too have an inward and an outward component. Together, these chapters should provide a framework in which to understand global issues and from which to act in response to basic human needs.

Moral Development Theory

Given what one reads daily in the papers, it may seem grandiose to claim that we human beings are, in fact, moral beings. Yet we could never make judgments about our actions and the conduct of others (and have these judgments validated) if we were not. Our very ability to question our morality affirms its presence. So where does moral decision-making come from, and how does it grow and develop within the individual?

A recent film from Argentina, *The Official Story,* moves toward an answer to that question. The film recounts the moral history of an upper middle-class woman, married to a prominent businessman, who has managed to survive a military-to-civilian change in government with his job intact.

The protagonist is tortured by the fact that she has never been able to have children. Some four or five years before the time of the film, her husband had presented her with a child for adoption, a child that he said had been unwanted by its mother and whose adoption had been arranged for by a helpful physician. The wife, a loving and generous woman, is quite happy until she renews acquaintance with an old friend who, in the early days of the military regime, had dated a Marxist, been imprisoned, and witnessed the stealing of babies from female political prisoners.

Fear enters the adopted mother's heart. Could little Gaby be one of these stolen babies? Why has her husband been so silent about the events that surrounded his receiving of the child? At the same time that she experiences intense personal fear, the woman begins to notice, for the first time, the presence of the Co-madres (mothers of the disappeared who demonstrate daily, asking for information about their loved ones) and other dissident voices. She begins to see some of the fear, poverty, and oppression that have surrounded her small, protected world all her life.

The woman is compelled by this crisis to think beyond self-interest and social conditioning. She is forced to think not only about Gaby's origin as the child of a young prisoner and the grand-child of a Co-madre, but also about oppression at large and the way it destroys relationships and nations. The protagonist moves *through* moral quandary and *out* into society at large.

Following a violent confrontation with her husband over his unwillingness to acknowledge the meaning of Gaby's history, she goes to join her daughter at the home of her open-minded, working class in-laws, leaving her door keys dangling in the lock. Her exit from her husband's home is proof not only that she has gone beyond his level of moral reasoning but that she has also found a larger world in which she must begin to live.

Clearly, this is a film about moral growth. We watch the protagonist change and mature in the way she sees and responds to the world. Always a "decent" woman, she becomes more intentionally, actively concerned about questions of human dignity, and we both admire her courage and wonder about the process.

One of the most widely accepted theories about moral process in our time is the cognitive-developmental approach to socialization of the late Lawrence Kohlberg. His work is based on the work of Jean Piaget and has been helpfully amended by Carol Gilligan. Basically, it describes sequential levels of moral thinking engaged in by human beings as they mature. In Kohlberg's most famous and definitive study, he interviewed a group of male subjects every three years over an eighteen year period, using a series of problem cases to elicit not only moral choices, but also the reasoning behind these choices. A typical problem case is that of Heinz whose wife was ill with cancer:

> In Europe, a woman was near death from cancer. One drug might save her, a form of radium that a druggist in the same town had recently discovered. The druggist was charging $2,000, ten times what the drug cost him to make. The sick woman's husband, Heinz, went to everyone he knew to borrow the money, but he could only get together about half of what it cost. He told the druggist that his wife was dying and asked him to sell it cheaper or let him pay later. But the druggist said, "No." The husband got desperate and broke into the man's store to steal the drug for his wife. Should the husband have done that? Why? ("Stage and Sequence" 379)

Interviewing his subjects from childhood into young adulthood, Kohlberg found that their moral decisions fell into six sequential stages which can be condensed into three general categories of moral reasoning:

I. Pre-conventional reasoning—decisions are made on the basis of personal well-being.

    Stage 1. "Action motivated by avoidance of punishment."

    Stage 2. "Action motivated by desire for reward or benefit."

II. Conventional reasoning—decisions are made on the basis of an individual's conformity with what is expected of his/her social groups.

    Stage 3. "Action motivated by anticipation of disapproval of others, actual or imagined-hypothetical (e.g. guilt)."

    Stage 4. "Action motivated by anticipation of dishonor, i.e., institutionalized blame for failure of duty, and by guilt over concrete harm done to others."

III. Post-conventional reasoning—decisions are made on the basis of universal principles.

Stage 5. "Concern about maintaining respect of equals and of the community (assuming their respect is based on reason rather than emotions)."

Stage 6. "Concern about self-condemnation for violating one's own principles." ("Stage and Sequence" 381–82)

According to Kohlberg's findings, the stages are followed in sequential order; one may regress from time to time in his or her development, particularly in periods of stress, but no stages are skipped. Each stage represents a new way of looking at and responding to the world and is more complex than the stage before. He also found that most people remain at stage four; stages five and six, especially six, are unusual as consistent patterns of moral decision making. Nonetheless they often provide the ideals by which a society, or group of persons seeks to define itself.

In *Moral Development: A Guide to Piaget and Kohlberg,* Ronald Duska and Mariellen Whelan make some helpful comments on the nature of stage development. They point out that persons have trouble understanding moral reasoning that takes place more than one stage beyond their own, yet are quite attracted to reasoning at the next stage. When strong discomfort occurs at the present stage, they will move to the stage of attraction. In addition, Duska and Whelan point out that movement through the first to fourth stages is characterized by "a more adequate perception of what the social system [is]," while stages five and six involve an understanding of "principles to which the society and the self *ought* to be committed" (968). That is, one moves from acceptance of conventional standards to an ability to call convention into question. Finally, Duska and Whelan point out that, for Kohlberg, justice is the highest principle toward which the whole process yearns. They would add love (justice *and* love), thus anticipating and accommodating Carol Gilligan's respectful criticism of Kohlberg.

Gilligan is a psychologist who, having worked and written

with Lawrence Kohlberg at Harvard, eventually published *In a Different Voice* (1982) in which she points out that by limiting himself to male adolescent subjects, Kohlberg has missed out on some very marked differences between the moral reasoning of men and women. When ignored, these differences relegate women to immature status in the hierarchy of moral development stages.

Utilizing comparative studies of male and female respondents, and drawing upon the studies of a number of other psychologists, Gilligan illustrates that male socialization focuses on separation and competition, while women's socialization stresses connection and community. (She notes that even in childhood play, boys will argue strenuously over whether a ball in baseball is fair or foul, while girls will often cease playing a game when conflict occurs in order to save relationships.) As they mature, males become concerned with hierarchy and women with networking. Men tend to develop toward an ethic of justice and women toward an ethic of care. Yet since the stages of moral development have traditionally been defined by studies with males, morally mature women who opt for responsibility and relationship seem to be stuck on the conventional level of moral reasoning, while morally mature men who opt for abstract principle score on the *post*-conventional level.

Gilligan is quick to assert in her preface that she is not discussing male and female per se, but male and female *voices,* both of which sound in most of us, and ought to. Yet in a world that desperately needs dialogue between separation and connection, justice and care, principles and responsibilities, psychological studies have tended to silence the "female" voice by opting for the "male" voice as normal development.

Carol Gilligan would have us consider morality, particularly post-conventional morality, in a more inclusive sense, recognizing the *interdependence* of an "ethic of justice [that] proceeds from the premise of equality" and an "ethic of care [that] rests on the premise of nonviolence" (174). She argues that a dialogue between justice and care at the highest levels of moral reasoning can only enhance each, and enlarge the whole. Thus, a true sense of justice would have to include responsible love, and no ethic of care could prosper without a respect for equal rights.

The Implications of Moral Development Theory for Basic Needs Concerns

There are a number of ways in which moral development theory complements the concerns of basic needs programs, programs geared toward providing all persons with clean water, sanitation, food, shelter, health services, education, participation in the political process, etc. Moral development theory is based on the responses of individuals to the world. It recognizes the necessary link between thought and action. Especially if one takes Carol Gilligan seriously, it stresses the complementarity of emotional and mental development. In short, it encourages wholeness.

√ It is our premise, as stated in the preface, that only a whole person cares about the wholeness of the world and about others in the world. But there are different levels of wholeness. Each stage of moral reasoning has a completeness to it—decisions "fit" with how a person sees the world. Yet after a while, disequilibrium may set in, motivating movement to the next stage. For example, I may be legitimately content for some time to give money to a lunch program in Haiti based on the fact that my church supports the program and I support my church. Eventually, however, I may begin to investigate the needs of the people for myself and decide to give on the basis of these understood needs. I will have moved into a larger, more complex world of moral concerns.

Gilligan's revision of the post-conventional stages of moral development is particularly helpful to a basic needs program in that it adds caring to justice. Ultimately, one does not respond to needs in the abstract, but to persons in need for whom one chooses to take responsibility.

Theoretically, then, there is evidence that a consideration of moral development enhances discussion of global ethics. But in a practical sense, how might one utilize the method of inquiry in order to come closer to one's own sensibilities and choices?

All of the cases Piaget and Kohlberg present to their subjects involve personal moral dilemmas. What if one were to reason about an "altruistic" act of generosity?

Many of us watched the Live Aid concert(s) in July 1985. Simultaneously, rock musicians and their fans flocked to Wembley Stadium in London and J.F.K. Stadium in Philadelphia in order to raise money for world hunger, specifically the famine in Ethiopia. Using Kohlberg's stages, with insights provided by Gilligan's research, let's look at possible reasons why particular rock stars might have played the benefit. Remember that the "content" and language of these stages may change according to an individual's belief system, but the *type* of reasoning will remain relatively constant.

PRE-CONVENTIONAL (individual concerns)
1. (fear of punishment) "All the other members of my band are going to do it. They might find another drummer if I refuse."
2. (personal gratification) "It'll be awesome! Just like Woodstock!"

CONVENTIONAL (societal concerns)
3. (approval) "The fans will love a rock star who is willing to give up a few bucks to feed starving children."
4. (honor/reputation) "People are unfairly suspicious of rock musicians. Let's show them that we care as much as anyone."

POST-CONVENTIONAL (universal concerns)
5. (respect for/maintenance of the community) "I should help to feed these people because I would want them to do the same for me."
6. (justice and care) "As a person who has enough to eat, I must insure this right to others. We *are* the world; their pain is ours."

Hopefully this "case" helps us to move from a situation demanding action to a choice to take "unnecessary," moral action. But since most of us are not rock musicians, nor do large scale benefit concerts occur regularly, let's look at a situation that could involve any of us, any time.

Suppose that a family of resettled Vietnamese refugees has moved in down the block. They can get by on charitable aid from churches and civic groups, but they'd prefer to work in self-sustaining jobs. To do this, they need to learn English. One could decide to tutor them for a number of reasons:

PRE-CONVENTIONAL (individual concerns)
1. (fear of punishment) "I know that we are supposed to help one another. If I don't do this, something bad may happen to me."
2. (personal gratification) "This will make me feel like a generous person."

CONVENTIONAL (social concerns)
3. (approval) "My neighbors will think I am really a good person if I do this."
4. (honor/reputation) "This is an act of good citizenship. Our country has always helped foreigners to integrate into the culture."

POST-CONVENTIONAL (universal concerns)
5. (respect for/maintenance of the community) "These people *deserve* a full life here, given what they have suffered. I owe these people a chance to live on their own, rather than endure the embarrassment of charity."
6. (justice and care) "Justice involves an equal chance to earn one's living. If I wish to be fully human, I cannot ignore the needs of this family."

In any case, the job gets done, and the success of the decision to help will produce contentment, but there's little doubt that the more altruistic, the more self-less the motive, the wider will be its sphere of influence and application. Justice and care take in more considerations than simple obedience to social conscience, and they endure longer. But it may take all of us a while to get to the point where we consistently elect projects on these bases. This in no way negates the work we do along the way.

It should also be noted that what the respondents are considering in this test case is not crisis relief aid but the supplying of a basic need (education) which eventually allows the recipients the dignity of their own sustenance.

The Development of Global Morality

The transition from conventional (stages three and four) to post-conventional (stages five and six) moral reasoning is a crucial one for the consideration of global ethics, because it is here that an individual moves from reliance on social factors to a faith in principles and human relationships that has the power to judge societies. Kohlberg describes a median stage (four and a half) characterized by skepticism, egoism and relativism. In this stage, the individual becomes aware that the social order is made up of pluralistic moral values, many of them based on expediency, and that he or she must look for a moral *center* elsewhere.

Stage four and a half correlates interestingly with Erik Erikson's stage five of human growth—adolescence—where identity is the key issue. Typically, the adolescent goes through a crisis of separation from accepted standards and seeks something to which to commit his or her life. That commitment might be to a deeper understanding of contextual norms or to values that question the norms, but to have no separation crisis is abnormal. (So-called "initiation rites" in a number of cultures recognize and support this need.)

Stage four and a half in moral development does not, of course, have to take place in adolescence, but it is experientially like adolescence. (Actually, most reorientations of identity and moral reasoning that we go through recall adolescence, which, because of its physiological, psychological, and role-expectancy factors, is the most intense transformation most of us goes through.) Stage four and a half, like our teenage years, can be frightening and very exciting. As an adolescent, one may discover that "home values" are not "world values" and that intelligent, principled moral choices are both possible and necessary. As a globally-conscious adult, one may discover that all that one thought was good and fine about his or her nation's foreign aid plan is but gloss on protection of special interests. What action, then, gives integrity to the human community? In such a quandary (a stage four and a half quandary) growth becomes necessary if one does not want to sink into the paralysis of cynicism.

Yet growth must continue both in moral development *and* in

the spheres to which one applies moral reasoning, if one is to remain fully alive. Let's consider for a moment the phenomenon of mid-life crisis. Why does it occur? It occurs for a variety of reasons, of course, which we cannot possibly rehearse here, but one may be able to generalize that much mid-life depression is a crisis of meaning emanating from the painful observation that one's world is too small. An individual may have learned to be successful and compassionate in a world that contains business, church, home and community, but have little cognizance of and care for what transpires elsewhere. He or she has a strong sense of self and of others but needs a wider sphere in which to "practice." For example, a teacher may have put in ten or twenty years motivating students to see the internal beauties of English literature, only to discover mid-career the wider beauty of the literary *process*. At this point, what has happened and is happening in the world becomes immensely important to his or her teaching. The fact that many persons become global citizens in middle age is not only unsurprising, it is logical and provides a wonderful base for global action programs.

What we are talking about here is how persons go about "moving out" in their moral applications as well as "moving through" the stages of moral development. These are complementary but not necessarily synonymous movements. (One can find hermits at stage five and missionaries at stage two.) But, more often than not, they motivate one another. Discovering the magnitude of global poverty stimulates thought about how and why we should respond. Heightened moral thinking stimulates the broadening of horizons. One bias that may need to be overcome for this combined development to take place on a larger scale is the way that people view altruism. It is a suspect quality in our pragmatic day, pertaining to ancient saints and bleeding heart liberals. Yet Mother Teresa's name stays reverently on everyone's lips. Is it possible that we are self-consciously suspicious of the very things we long for because we no longer think they are possible?

In an article entitled "Educating for a Just Society: An Updated and Revised Statement" (1980), Lawrence Kohlberg argues for public and private school education aimed at stage four moral reasoning, having given up his previous goal of education for stages six and five. Why this shrinking of expectations? In the same article, he makes a nostalgic comment about the climate of life in the United States two decades ago:

> In the sixties, we seemed to see youth groping toward principled fifth or even sixth stage reasoning, and recoiling from fourth stage political leadership while being misunderstood as immoral and lawless. (463)

In contrast to the sixties, Kohlberg explains, youth in the late seventies "are responding to an overwhelming national mood of privatism," which makes stage four a significant goal (460).

Yes, social emphases change, but if we would be globally responsible people, we need to avoid lowest common denominators and to reach for complexity of ethical thinking, as well as breadth of concern. The two considerations come together in another recent film, *Platoon*, which has been praised for "telling it like it was" in Vietnam. In this film a middle-class, white college student drops out of school and enlists in the army, requesting Vietnam. Why? Even he isn't sure. Curiosity is a factor, as is his vaguely conscientious response to the accusation that the poor, the uneducated, and the blacks are fighting this war for the rest.

He finds that all is as he suspected—even worse. The arguments at home over the morality/immorality of the conflict are embodied in two warring sergeants of the platoon. Although the blacks like him, they find his enlistment bizarre. In addition, the carnage is far worse than anything he imagined.

The young man's personal pain and confusion become intense, but he learns to see things in a new way. He sees that the struggle of the black soldiers is real, emanates from inequality at home, and relates to the cheapness of "yellow life" in this and many wars. He sees that the struggle between the sergeants is real, emanates from a moral struggle inherent in the way this war has evolved, and relates to guerrilla warfare in general.

He moves out of his vague discomfort into intense discomfort, and finally chooses to take violent action against the offensively hawkish sergeant. Many viewers may disagree with his choice of actions, but it illustrates his growing sense that life-saving decisions *must* be made and that they affect not only the integrity of the

individual but the integrity of the human community. The mentality of the sergeant has led to nothing but wholesale death and racial
hatred—it must be confronted.

One might say the protagonist has gained vision. Vision, and
its attendant power to motivate action, is greatly needed in our
world. James Fowler addresses this need when he compares Kohlberg's moral stages to the development of faith. He criticizes Kohlberg for being too rational in his methodology, claiming that faith
is a *condition* and motivation for moral judgment. Without faith in
that which is not yet present, or commitment to change, moral
reasoning is an academic phrase. As Fowler sees it, a moral stage is
"a particular *way* of organizing, composing, or of giving form to
the contents of beliefs or values" (143). In like spirit, he defines
faith as a matter of creating an image of the perfect environment
and committing oneself to the values that give this image coher-
ence and empower its realization.

It is obvious that one can have ethics without organized religion, but can one have ethics without faith and commitment—
those factors which energize values and force them into concrete
action? Carol Gilligan, while not calling it faith, certainly argues
for a primary connectedness that needs to be preserved in moral
development. Even with Kohlberg's insistence on cognition, faith
in and commitment to justice seem to lie beyond and motivate
moral reasoning in his theory (causing him to posit a possible stage
seven).

Related fields follow suit. In an article entitled "Obstacles to
World Development: An Ethical Reflection," Denis Goulet points
out that social scientists writing on development issues are beginning to use the word "transcendence" in their works, belatedly
acknowledging the importance of visionary thinking to the fulfillment of social change. He also points out that persons working for
change on the grassroots level have understood the validity of
intuitive thinking and belief for some time.

Suffice it to say, we are all motivated by *something* to reason
and act morally in the world. It is the same "thing" that causes us
to create ethical systems. Call it a universal compulsion if you like,
or a transcendent goal, or faith, or God's call. But do not praise
Mother Teresa and deny its possibility. We are thinking, feeling,

contextual beings with a capacity to see with love, contemplate just systems, and commit ourselves to such visions and contemplation. Perhaps it is growth itself, an *unfolding* of justice and love, that inspires our visions. And perhaps it is only by validating our own human dignity through the process of taking our moral development (and its causes) seriously that we can hope to achieve a world where human dignity is universally valued.

Yet where will this individual hope take us if not into a consideration of collective values? Chapter Two looks at how four of our major cultural systems evaluate human dignity, both in terms of moral obligations to persons within the community *and* to persons who remain outside. Hopefully, by the end of Chapter Two it will be clear that while systems shape individual values, it is the ethical questions of thinking individuals that can redeem and reorder our collective experience.

BIBLIOGRAPHY

Duska, Ronald and Mariellen Whelan. *Moral Development: A Guide to Piaget and Kohlberg.* New York: Paulist Press, 1975.

Erikson, Erik H. *Identity: Youth and Crisis.* New York: W.W. Norton, 1968.

Fowler, James. "Moral Stages and the Development of Faith," *Moral Development, Moral Education, and Kohlberg,* edited by Brenda Munsey. Birmingham, Alabama: Religious Education Press, 1980.

Gilligan, Carol. *In a Different Voice.* Cambridge: Harvard University Press, 1982.

Goulet, Denis. "Obstacles to World Development: An Ethical Reflection," *World Development,* Vol. 11, No. 7 (July 1983).

Kohlberg, Lawrence. "Stage and Sequence: The Cognitive-developmental Approach to Socialization," *Handbook of Socialization Theory and Research,* edited by David A. Goslin. Chicago: Rand McNally, 1969.

———. "Educating for a Just Society: An Updated and Revised Statement," *Moral Development, Moral Education, and Kohlberg,* edited by Brenda Munsey. Birmingham, Alabama: Religious Education Press, 1980.

SUGGESTIONS FOR FURTHER STUDY

Fowler, James, and Sam Keen. *Life Maps: Conversations in the Journey of Faith.* Waco, Texas: Word Books, 1978.

Gilligan, Carol. *In a Different Voice.* Cambridge: Harvard University Press, 1982.

Kohlberg, Lawrence. *Stages in the Development of Moral Thought and Action.* New York: Holt, Rinehart, and Winston, 1969.

Mussen, Paul H. and Nancy Eisenberg-Berg. *Roots of Caring, Sharing and Helping.* San Francisco: W.H. Freeman and Company, 1977.

Shue, Henry. *Basic Rights: Subsistence, Affluence, and U.S. Foreign Policy.* Princeton: Princeton University Press, 1980.

DISCUSSION QUESTIONS AND ACTIVITIES

1. If each member of your group was given $1,000 to "invest" in the charitable cause of his or her choice, where would the money go, and why? Discuss the choices in terms of breadth of moral concern as well as nature of moral reasoning.

2. Take some time to talk about your own moral education. As each of you was growing up, what persons and experiences brought you into awareness of the needs of others? What persons and experiences "turned you off" to "goodness"? What have been the major moral crises of your lives to date? What do you suspect will be moral crises in the future? Do you discern any patterns here?

3. Take a few minutes for each person to jot down the core-beliefs that inform his or her moral reasoning. Then share these beliefs. Where do they come from? How do they influence moral reasoning? (Urge one another to give concrete examples; continue the story-telling you began with #2.)

4. Ask yourselves what it is that motivates children to share. Analyze these motives. Then, as a group, design a program to educate children to be more responsive to the needs of others.

5. Using the Live Aid concert(s) and tutoring for Vietnamese refugees as guides, design a test case that pertains to the inter-

ests of your group. Write out your responses to the problem individually, then share them and discuss the varieties of motivation represented. Which motivations will lead to the most sustained action? Which motivations will lead to the widest sphere of action?

6. Read quickly over your response journals and discuss special concerns raised there.

2

Rediscovering Human Dignity
Through Global Perspectives

In the modern world, reality is perceived to be divided into polar opposites. Among the more common manifestations of this polarization are dichotomies between science and religion in philosophy, realism, and romanticism in literature, and materialism and idealism in sociology. Everywhere one can see examples, yet one dichotomy which has received little treatment is that between tribalism and universalism in cultural systems.

Tribal*ism* (not to be confused with the cultures of "primitive" or traditional societies) is the tendency to see one's social group as the central fact or final aim of the universe, and to interpret reality exclusively in terms of that social group. Universalism, in contrast, is the tendency to see the world as a whole and to interpret one's existence in relation to that larger community. The present tension between nationalism and globalism reflects this dichotomy.

The modern world is essentially tribalistic. Intense nationalism dominates the political arena, and individuals are usually identified by their nationality. For example, on the brink of World War II, the United States built concentration camps for Japanese-Americans, assuming that, being native Japanese, their primary loyalties would be with their mother nation. The distinction was made on the basis of ethnic origin, not behavior or political ideology. At the same time that such events have shaped our recent history, however, we have maintained a rhetoric of universalism, speaking of "good neighbor policies" and "global villages."

The same discrepancy defines our ideas of poverty. If we are to be effective in responding to world poverty, which is the hope of this study, it is necessary for us to reclaim an understanding of the essential dignity of *all* persons. Yet, in reality, poverty is often perpetuated by a tribalistic mentality, both of the poor and the non-poor. The poor often believe that because they are of a particular neighborhood or country, of a particular race, or of a particular educational background, they are powerless to climb out of their poverty. Thus the poor see themselves forever tied to their social class (a tribalistic mentality). Meanwhile, the non-poor often believe that while the poor deserve occasional acts of charity, they are essentially responsible for their position outside of society. Denying the poor access to the community of the non-poor is then justifiable in light of their lack of motivation.

To further understand the reality and cause of this divisive consciousness, we need to examine the tension between tribalism and universalism in our prominent religious and secular systems. By doing so, we will come to see that while tribalism may be the "norm" in our current cultural systems, universalism is at the core of each.

Tribalism and Universalism in Religious Systems

Tribalism in the Judaic Tradition

> And I will make you a great nation, and I will bless you and make your name great, and you will be a blessing . . . and through you all of the nations of the earth shall be blessed.
>
> *Genesis 12:2–3*

German sociologist Max Weber in *Ancient Judaism* characterizes the Jewish people as "a pariah people, which means . . . that they were a guest people who were ritually separated, formally or de facto, from their social surroundings" (3). In terms of ancient Israel's geographical location, their retreat into cultural separatism is understandable. The small country was situated between various antagonistic cultures, the Egyptians to the southwest, the Assyrians in the north, and the Babylonians to the east. They feared both invasion and religious corruption, and because they were a distinct minority they were perceived as outcasts. During their many periods of exile, including their long pilgrimage in Europe, the Jews remained culturally distinct, living in ghettos by both choice and force.

In the modern world, Jewish separatism or "pariahism" may be most readily manifested in the conservative Hasidic tradition. Hasidic Jews, with their simple and unobtrusive style of dress and their refusal to embrace such western conventions as the use of electricity or any mechanical devices on the sabbath, can be seen as a people who have set themselves apart from western society. Like the ancient Jews, the Hasids attempt to preserve the purity of Jewish monotheism from idolatry, whether it be of pagan gods or material goods.

Ancient Jews further demonstrated their tribalistic tendencies in their formulation of a doctrine of messianic nationalism. This doctrine had at its core the belief that the Jews were the chosen people of God, the anointed ones, and that they were to inherit a land promised to them. Concerning this, Weber says, "What mattered to Yahweh was Israel alone, as was, after all, expected at all times of every local god, or local saint, and every localized madonna" (134). This belief led to the conception of Yahweh as a mighty warrior, as one who fought for Israel.

The Israelites manifested this idea of Yahweh in various ways such as the belief that the God of Israel indwelt the ark of the covenant, as well as the sacred tabernacle. (See Numbers 10:35–36 and 1 Samuel 1:9, 4:4, in conjunction with the image presented in Jeremiah 3:16.) This notion naturally led to Israel's belief in themselves as a people chosen by God, which was used to justify such activities as the slaughter of the non-Yawistic nations (Deuteronomy 7:1–26) and usuriousness (excessive interest gathering) against these same nations.

Modern Zionism in the middle east today is clearly a continuation, if a partial secularization, of this long-held belief in the nation's chosenness.

Universalism in the Judaic Tradition

Universalism, as has been stated, is at the core of Judaism. This is most apparent in the doctrine of *imago dei* (that human beings are created in the image of God), and the early Judaic tradition that Israel was the vehicle through which all nations would be blessed.

✓ The doctrine of *imago dei* is foundational to historic Judaism. At the heart of the doctrine is an affirmation of the essential dignity of human beings based upon a belief that human beings are created in the image of God. Historic Judaism understands in a way which modern secular persons do not that humans express a profound degree of similarity to the divine. Far from being applied solely to the worshipers of Yahweh, the concept of *imago dei* was extended universally to non-Yahwists. Furthermore, Jewish theologian David Shapiro suggests that the doctrine of *imago dei* is inseparably linked with the ethical mandate of *imitatio dei* (that human beings should imitate God):

> That *imitatio dei* is a genuine concept is evident from the fact that the imperative of holiness, whether applied to Israelites or to priests, is consistently motivated by the holiness of God (Lev. 11:44; 19:2; 20:26; 21:8). God loves the stranger; therefore the children of Israel are to love the stranger (Deut. 10:18, 19). (128)

The idea of the universalistic and normative nature of *imago dei* (and *imitatio dei*) is attested to by the fact that ancient Judaism allowed for the admittance of certain non-Israelites, termed the "god-fearers," into the faith. Were it not for Judaism's belief in the normative value of *imago dei* for all human beings, such an occurrence would have been unlikely, and Judaism might have dwindled as a cultural system. The application of this doctrine by the Jews was motivated by a universalism which, in turn, reinforced the positive advance and perpetuation of Judaism itself.

Universalism was further manifest in the belief that the Jews were to be the vehicles through which God would bless all nations:

> Biblical Judaism conceived of God as universal, but as choosing Israel as the instrument for his transcending truth, therefore consigning his chosen people to con-

tumely and pain until all the nations would recognize its
role in history as the teacher of mankind. (Gordis 23)

The promise made to the patriarch Abraham, father of the Israelites, was not merely that he and his descendants would be blessed,
but that *through* him "all the nations of the world will be blessed"
(Genesis 12:3). Israel was to be distinguished not because they
were superior to other nations but because they stood in covenant
with Yahweh and because through them Yahweh would bring the
others into covenant.

It may be argued that it was never Yahweh's will that Israel
become a nation insulated against attempts at penetration by other
nations. Such a separatist retreat from the world would be restric-
tively tribalistic, not at all in keeping with Israel's universalistic
mission.

Tribalism in Christianity

Early Christianity maintained a rigid distinction between "the
church" and "the world." By "the church" early Christians meant
the body of believers in Jesus Christ; "the world" was used to
designate the unbelieving multitudes who were, because of their
unbelief, "lost." While this distinction was not an inherently
tribalistic one—due to the fact that early Christianity possessed a
controlling belief that it had a mission to convert "the world" and
integrate them into "the church"—it is quite possible that it facili-
tated the growth of tribalism.

For example, gnosticism, an early influence in Christianity,
maintained a rigid distinction between the possessors of true knowledge and the uninitiated. The former were those who through
extreme asceticism, or other means, were granted a mystical union
with pure knowledge leading to salvation. It was a union which was
not guaranteed to everyone and, as such, functioned as a *technique
of separation,* creating and perpetuating a distinction between a
gnostic elite—the possessors of knowledge—and those without
knowledge of salvation.

Early Christianity embodied a second form of tribalism in
what Paul called "the Judaizers." The work of the Judaizers was

directed at bringing Gentile converts into conformity with the Jewish rites of circumcision and the dietary prohibitions against eating food sacrificed to idols, or meat which had been strangled or was eaten with blood. The attempt of the Judaizers to gain Gentile conformity to Jewish rites is a form of tribalism manifesting the *technique of symbolic distinction.*

Modern Christianity has also proven to be susceptible to the forces of tribalism. Two periods, in particular, embody this tribalism; the Puritanism of early America and the defensive separatism of today's "religious right" and "religious left."

The Puritans inherited from the Israelites a belief in the specialness of their relationship to God. Like the Jews they believed themselves to be a chosen people. This perception manifested itself in their segregationist treatment of native Americans, for it perpetuated the *a priori* judgment of the Puritans that the Indians, unlike themselves, did not possess souls.

A more contemporary example of the tribalistic tendencies of modern Christianity is the defensive separatism which characterizes both the "religious right" and the "religious left." Among the "religious right" there is a tendency to retreat into pietistic groups, which produces two noticeable effects. The first is the "huddle-effect" wherein believers of identical dogma huddle together to insulate themselves from the numbing wind of modernism raging throughout society. The second is the "pariah effect," a nascent belief that they are outsiders, which results in an attitude of defensive self-righteousness.

Among the "religious left" there is a similar separatism. While the "religious left" exhibits meritorious tolerance toward secularism, feminism, atheism and the religious pluralism of non-Christian belief systems, it is notorious for its intolerance of Christian fundamentalism. There is a unifying sentiment among members of the "religious left" that the execution of the Christian faith in the form prescribed by those of the "right" is irrelevant and simple-minded.

Universalism in Christianity

The universalism of the Christian tradition is expressed in the incarnation. The fact that Jesus comes as a person of meager circumstances, and of seeming insignificance, identifies him with the *least* of humanity; therefore he becomes a symbol of *all* humanity. In the same vein, the concept of universalism is suggested in Jesus' baptism. The baptism which John preached was a baptism of repentance and was, if one accepts the belief that Christ was sinless, unnecessary for Jesus. Nevertheless, the scriptures record that Jesus underwent baptism by John. Why, if not in order to identify himself with the human condition? Thus, when Jesus at his baptism is proclaimed to be the faithful Son of God, it is a simultaneous affirmation to people of the earth that they too are God's children.

Finally, the death and subsequent resurrection of Jesus are universal affirmations of humanity. In Christian liturgies all over the world, Jesus is celebrated as the universal sacrifice, the "lamb of God who takes away the sin of the world" (John 1:29). Furthermore, the death of Jesus is an affirmation of God's solidarity with human suffering. Jesus experiences suffering and loss because human beings suffer. Moreover, having suffered the shame of the crucifixion, Jesus dies and thus completes his identification with mortal humanity. This, however, is not God's final word. According to the gospels, Jesus is resurrected three days following his death—a symbol of God's acceptance both of Jesus and of all humanity.

Beyond the central figure of its messiah, the Christian tradition manifests universalism through its choice of earthly saints and heroes. Within the New Testament one finds the faith of soldiers, lepers, prostitutes, and tax collectors upheld as examples for imitation. To these poor and disenfranchised persons Jesus preached the promise of the kingdom of God and claimed that they were its heirs. Jesus attacked the attitude that such persons were relegated to their low position in society because they were not "blessed by God." The kingdom of God was to be a universal society.

The ethical teachings of Jesus, like his life and associations with base humanity, manifest the universalism of the Christian tradition. Within much of the Bible there is the suggestion that correct conduct and an execution of justice for the oppressed is a form of divine worship. This suggestion is elaborated in the New Testament, especially concerning Jesus' teachings on the proper treatment of one's neighbor. In his sermon on the mount, Jesus boldly challenges the popular saying, "You shall love your neighbor and hate your enemies," by saying, "But I say to you, love your enemies and pray for those who persecute you" (Matthew 5:43–44). Furthermore, Jesus asserts (Mark 12:29–31) that the Mosaic mandate to "love your neighbor as yourself" (Leviticus 19:18) is practically identical to the sacred mandate known as the Shema: "Hear, O, Israel! The Lord is our God, the Lord is one! And you shall love the Lord your God with all your heart and with all your soul and with all your might" (Deuteronomy 6:4–5). To the young lawyer's question—"And who is my neighbor?"—Jesus answers with the parable of the good Samaritan, asserting that neighborliness crosses ethnic lines and negates long-term prejudice. Jesus adds to this parable the imperative, "Go and do likewise," indicating that entrance into the kingdom is predicated upon such imitation.

Tribalism and Universalism in Secular Systems

There has never been an age more secular than the modern age. Despite the reappearance of traditional religion, secularism has reigned triumphant on many fronts. Religion is no longer perceived as adequate to explain our biological origin. Furthermore, religious ideas no longer play an influential role in shaping our social theories or political ideologies (with the exception of Islamic fundamentalism). The modern mind receives a majority of its explanations from the combined sciences.

One thing that religious and secular systems share, however, is the tension between tribalism and universalism; and, ultimately, they share a concern for human dignity. We will investigate this tension and this concern in the systems of Marxism and capitalism.

Tribalism in Marxism

One can detect within Marx's writings a nascent tribalism. It is a tribalism which is formed by Marx's theory of class conflict, and is, to him, confirmed in experience.

According to Marx, the proletariat (working class) are united primarily by their common hatred of the bourgeoisie. This is developed in Marx and Engels' *Manifesto of the Communist Party* where it states, "The proletariat goes through various stages of development. With its birth begins its struggle with the bourgeoisie" (*Basic Writings* 15). Furthermore, the goals of the proletariat are the violent overthrow of the bourgeoisie. All revolutions by the proletariat will succeed or fail based upon the success or failure of the proletariat to organize itself around its common hatred of the bourgeoisie (capitalist class). That this is tribalistic is undeniable.

The organization of the working class around its hatred of the capitalist class is not the only manifestation of Marxist tribalism, however. A second example comes through Marx's suggestion that the proletariat is a "chosen class": ". . . because its [the proletariat's] suffering is universal . . . it can only emancipate itself by emancipating itself from all other classes and, thereby, emancipating them all" (265). Jules Monnerot attests to this claim when he states that the alienation of the working class will only be overcome by "the action of that class whose present abasement reveals it as the chosen class" (42). The overthrow of the bourgeoisie is considered by Marx to be the historic *mission* of the proletariat and will culminate in a single world-emancipating act (*Basic Writings* 264).

These tribalistic suggestions within Marx's writings are covert and subtle, however, in comparison with modern communism. One observes within the writings of Lenin a modification of the theories of Marx, especially in terms of his understanding of the proletariat. In "What Is To Be Done," Lenin states that the working class has failed to develop a belief that the social abuses of the bourgeoisie can be overcome by a revolutionary movement (122). They are trapped inside their belief that they can only reform the existing social order through strikes and minor revolts. Because of this, Lenin advocates a "dictatorship of the proletariat" by a "revolutionary socialist intelligentsia" (122).

This intelligentsia is necessarily a minority group within the social order. According to Lenin, the purpose of this group is to rule over the proletariat, interpret its present needs, and disseminate education, until the time when the proletariat can seize control of the means of production. It is easy to see how such a program of leadership could become abusive. Within Soviet communism, this abuse has taken the form of privilege among the members of the communist party, who comprise a mere ten percent of the Soviet citizenry. Privilege is manifested in the simple fact that members of the communist party can go directly to the front of waiting lines for items difficult to obtain. Furthermore, party members receive better apartments and easier access to higher education than the general populace. Thus one can see that the communism of Lenin and, subsequently, modern Soviet communism is an exchange of bourgeois rule for rule by the revolutionary socialist elite. In this sense, it is a tribalistic vision.

Universalism in Marxism

Despite the degeneration of contemporary Marxism into overt tribalism, Marxism remains an essentially universalistic system. The universalism of Marx's vision is conveyed in the concepts of "the nationless proletariat," "the classless society" and "the borderless state." Originally, Marx's vision was of a unified body of workers who, through violent revolution, would depose the ruling bourgeoisie and seize control of the means of production. What is interesting to note is that Marx never identifies the proletariat with any particular nation. What distinguishes it as a class is not a particular nationality, but rather a common consensus concerning the abuses of the bourgeoisie.

Potentially the proletariat is any group whose common denominator is the oppression which it suffers at the hands of the capitalist class. Practically, it is the unified "workers of the world"—for communism can only be achieved through such unification (*Basic Writings* 41). The workers of the various nations must, according to Marx, form an international communist movement in order to rid the world of nations.

Marx's conception of the "classless society" forms the second aspect of his essential universalism. Within his vision is the belief that the result of the proletariat's activity will be a society with no class distinctions. Marx believes this will be accomplished through the abolition of oppressive forms of private ownership. According to Marx, once this has occurred, several things will take place. The first is the eradication of competition and the flowering of cooperation. Human beings will no longer compete for control of the means of production, for the structure of the communist system will make this impossible. Furthermore, human consciousness will evolve to such an extent that competition will appear foolish. Finally, the abolition of private ownership will remove from society the basis for class distinctions. According to Marx, class will no longer be determined by the distribution of wealth and distinctions in levels of consumption. The abolition of private property will thus make class distinctions an impossibility.

Finally, Marx and Engels convey their fundamental universalism in the concept of "the borderless state." After the proletariat has seized control of society and abolished private ownership and class distinctions, the state will generally "wither away," having become unnecessary. International communist workers will unite and promote insurgency throughout the world, absorbing the bourgeoisie into themselves. Thus capitalist states will be replaced by a classless, propertyless, international society whose members are economically indistinguishable from one another.

One may smile at the utopian idealism embodied in this scenario, but the vision has inspired a whole host of socio-political movements and theories. Chances are it will continue to do so.

Tribalism in Capitalism

As in the case of Marxism, capitalism contains within its basic assumptions concepts which, while not inherently tribalistic, have done much to foster tribalism. In Adam Smith's *The Wealth of Nations,* for example, Smith contends that "It is not from the benevolence of the butcher, the brewer, or the baker that we expect our dinner, but from their regard to their own interest" (15). Smith not only recognizes self-interest as a social fact, he also exalts it as the operative principle of capitalism. While no one would wish to contend with Smith's claim that self-interest is a reality, many would question his glorification of the concept based on the belief that the invisible hand of the market will hold self-interest in check and create a natural harmony of interests.

One wonders, in fact, whether the principle of self-interest operates in the way Smith describes, or whether it encourages just the opposite. When it is allowed to operate unchecked, self-interest seems to increase the gulf between the rich and the poor. This eventually decreases competition and stifles free enterprise, further concentrating wealth in the hands of a few. Laborers suspect owners, and owners commit themselves to defending and maintaining their advantage. Economically this creates rigid in-group/out-group distinctions which are symptomatic of tribalism.

A second concept of Smith's economic philosophy which deserves attention is that of the private ownership of property. Smith understood that "as soon as the land of any country has all become private property, the landlords, like all other men, love to reap where they never sowed, and demand a rent even for its natural produce" (47). What is interesting to note is that Smith does not critique this practice but rather accepts it as an operative principle and the natural right of the landowner. While it may appear that on a superficial level Smith is correct, it is also apparent that the unrestricted accumulation of private property can become oppressive. Society may divide into a class of oppressed laborers, who, because of present inequalities, will seek radical reform and redistribution of both property and capital, and a class of defensive and conservative landowners seeking the preservation of the status quo.

Perhaps no one has captured the tribalistic nature of this system better than Marx. Marx conceived that the concentration of property in private hands results in the alienation of human beings from their "species-being" and a retreat into individualism (*Basic Writings* 148). According to Marx this alienation occurs within the proletariat when workers do not have ownership and control of the means of production and thus are forced to sell their labor and become alienated from their work. It occurs between the proletariat and the bourgeoisie when, as a result of self-interest and profit motivation, persons amass large amounts of private property and exploit their workers, thus distancing themselves from a large segment of the population. As a result, competition rather than cooperation dominates the economic and social relationships of persons.

Another aspect of capitalism which encourages tribalism is that of privilege. Privilege, like property, is generally concentrated in the wealthy and withheld from the poor. While the vast majority of North Americans are aware that it is the right of all people to "reap private benefit from the use of the means of production and the right to utilize the dynamic forces of the marketplace for private enrichment," very few wish to recognize that in reality "the operative result [is] in favoring certain individuals and groups" (Heilbroner, *Limits* 71). Many believe that land, labor and capital are merely neutral factors in an impersonal and impartial market system.

Reality, however, paints a very different picture of modern capitalism. Heilbroner points out:

> . . . the operation of capitalism as *functional* system results in a structure of wealth and income characteristic of capitalism as a *system of privilege*—a structure in which the top two percent of all American families own between two-thirds and three-quarters of all corporate stock, and where the top two percent of all income receivers enjoy incomes roughly ten times larger than the average received within the nation as a whole. (72)

That such a system of privilege is tribalistic seems undeniable, for it creates a hierarchy of rigid socio-economic distinctions which paralyzes the initiative of the poor and creates defensiveness, suspicion, and capriciousness in the rich.

Universalism in Capitalism

When Adam Smith speaks of self-interest in *The Wealth of Nations*, it is not a negative concept. In fact, Smith believes that human self-interest will ultimately lead to a betterment of the human condition. This will be achieved by each person's active pursuit of self-interest in a free market economy, the result of which will create competition among producers for satisfied customers, which in turn will result in a competition to produce the greatest number of goods of the greatest quality for the lowest possible price. Thus Smith believes that an open market with extensive competition among producers (based on the principle of self-interest) allows the vast majority of people to reap the fruits of such competition, thus leading to the betterment of the individual as well as the society.

Such a vision is essentially universalistic in character, for it sees the improvement of humanity as the goal of economic competition. Even though the owners of enterprises may be motivated to hire thousands of workers in order to increase their own wealth, the workers will necessarily share in the improvements produced by their labors. One must therefore conclude, if one agrees with Smith's assumptions, that enlightened self-interest is not *fundamentally* destructive or tribalistic and is, in fact, a tremendous resource for human and social progress. It is this aspect of Smith's theory which is so compelling, for it maintains that the single most universal impulse of humans (self-interest) when exercised in a free market results in a dynamic movement of society toward socioeconomic justice and equality.

Another influence on the universalistic vision of capitalism comes through Calvinism. The first scholar to perceive the influence of Protestantism on the development of capitalism is German sociologist Max Weber. Weber's hypothesis is that the doctrines of Calvinism, which stress the industriousness of the Christian believer, as well as responsible stewardship, result in a spirit of industry on the one hand, and an accumulation of capital on the other. What makes these forces universalistic is Calvin's assertion that human beings are to be responsible stewards of the creation and to seek not personal gain but the material improvement of others. For Calvin the economic life is integrated with and inseparable from the moral life of humankind; the marketplace is where persons "prove" themselves.

A core belief of capitalism is that *all* will be the beneficiaries of free competition taking shape under the invisible hand of the market (sometimes seen in a theological light). This is its universalist claim. Whether or not such a condition is achievable, it remains the hopeful vision for many persons.

Throughout this chapter, we have investigated the various ways in which contemporary religious and secular systems embody the tension between universal and tribal interests. Furthermore, we have seen ways in which tribalistic distinctions, although important for group identity, prevent human beings from the identification of all people as fully and equally human. As long as such distinctions exist, the provision of basic human needs such as sufficient food, safe water, adequate shelter, education, protection from disease, and political freedom will continue to be an "ingroup" concern, but not a global concern. Human dignity will be accorded to certain persons, but not to others.

The challenge to each of us, as participants in these systems and as moral individuals, is to examine their universalistic roots, and to find ways to promote parity rather than hierarchy. We need to know the history, beliefs, and rituals of our assumed and/or chosen institutions, but we also need to rediscover within them the call to recognize and respond to the dignity of all persons. As the preface states, we must hold one another with equal respect, for justice emerges from such mutuality.

BIBLIOGRAPHY

Bennet, John C. *Christianity and Communism.* New York: Associated Press, 1951.

Cox, Harvey. *Religion in the Secular City.* New York: Simon and Schuster, 1984.

Dupre, Louis. *The Philosophical Foundations of Marxism.* New York: Harcourt, Brace and World, 1966.

Garaudy, Roger. *From Anathema to Dialogue,* translated by Luke O'Neill. New York: Herder and Herder, 1966.

Giddens, Anthony. *Capitalism and Modern Social Theory.* New York: Cambridge University Press, 1971.

Gordis, Robert. *The Root and the Branch.* Chicago: The University of Chicago Press, 1962.

Goudzwaard, Bob. *Capitalism and Progress,* translated by Josina Van Nuis Zylstra. Grand Rapids: Eerdmans Publishing Company, 1979.

Gutierrez, Gustavo. *A Theology of Liberation,* translated by Sister Caridad Inda and John Eagleson. New York: Orbis Books, 1973.

Heilbroner, Robert L. *The Limits of American Capitalism.* New York: Harper and Row, 1965.

———. *The Nature and Logic of Capitalism.* New York: W.W. Norton and Company. 1985.

Lenin, Vladimir I. *Lenin: Selected Works,* volume I. New York: International Publishers, 1967.

Marx, Karl. *Capital,* edited by Frederick Engels. New York: The Modern Library, 1906.

———. *The Economic and Philosophic Manuscripts of 1844,* edited by Dirk J. Struik and translated by Martin Milligan. New York: International Publishers, 1964.

———. *Early Writings,* translated by T.B. Bottomore. New York: McGraw-Hill, 1964.

Marx, Karl and Frederick Engels. *Basic Writings on Politics and Philosophy,* edited by Lewis S. Feuer. New York: Doubleday and Company, 1959.

———. *On Religion.* New York: Schocken Books, 1964.

Monnerot, Jules. *Sociology and Psychology of Communism,* translated by Jane Degras and Richard Rees. Boston: Beacon Press, 1960.

Raphael, D.D., editor. *British Moralists,* volume II. Oxford: Clarendon Press, 1969.

Shapiro, David S. "The Doctrine of the Image of God and Imitatio Dei," *Judaism.* Vol. 13, No. 1 (1963).

Smith, Adam. *The Theory of Moral Sentiments,* edited by D.D. Raphael and A.L. Macfie. New York: Oxford University Press, 1979.

———. *The Wealth of Nations,* edited by Bruce Maxlish. New York: Bobbs-Merrill Company, 1961.

Weber, Max. *Ancient Judaism,* translated and edited by Hans H. Gerth and Don Martindale. New York: The Free Press, 1952.

———. *The Protestant Ethic and the Spirit of Capitalism,* translated by Talcott Parsons. New York: Charles Scribner's Sons, 1958.

SUGGESTIONS FOR FURTHER STUDY

Bellah, Robert, et al. *Habits of the Heart: Individualism and Commitment in American Life.* Berkeley: University of California Press, 1985.

Goudzwaard, Bob. *Capitalism and Progress: A Diagnosis of Western Society*. Grand Rapids: Eerdmans, 1979.

Pemberton, Prentiss and Daniel Finn. *Toward a Christian Economic Ethic: Stewardship and Social Power*. Minneapolis: Winston Press, 1985.

Stackhouse, Max. *Creeds, Society and Human Rights: A Study in Three Cultures*. Grand Rapids: Eerdmans, 1984.

Wogaman, J. Phillip. *The Great Economic Debate: An Ethical Analysis*. Philadelphia: The Westminster Press, 1977.

DISCUSSION QUESTIONS AND ACTIVITIES

1. Think about the groups to which you belong and the ways in which they tend to be more centripetal (pulling in to the center) than centrifugal (reaching out to the circumference). Does this inward movement tend to make you feel secure or claustrophobic? Do you think it is essential to the group's identity? How do others outside the group view this?

2. To what extent are the groups to which you belong *in*clusive rather than *ex*clusive? How could they be even more inclusive?

3. To what extent do you think that people need "tribal" identities in order to be universalistic? Approach this discussion through the technique of storytelling—narrate events in which moving inward meant moving outward.

4. After each of you has read the chapter, but before you meet together, prepare a character sketch of the most "whole" person you know. (This would be a good journal exercise.) When you are together, share these portraits and then talk about the inclusiveness/exclusiveness of these people's lives.

5. Take a couple of moments to think about human dignity. What are its attributes? What people in the world do not appear to possess these attributes? Why don't they have them?

6. Read quickly over your journals and discuss important questions that appear there.

Part II

A Realistic Look at World Poverty

3

Physical Aspects of Poverty

We have all seen poverty. We all know of welfare families who huddle together in subsistence housing on cold winter nights. Most of us have seen the rural poor as well—children in Appalachia who are listless and pale and sleep five to a bed. But having seen all of that, we still do not know what absolute poverty is, that "condition of life so characterized by malnutrition, illiteracy and disease as to be beneath any reasonable definition of human decency" (*World Development Report, 1980* 32). There are nearly 800 million people in the world who are absolutely poor. Who are they?

Universally applicable standards are hard to define, but basically a person is considered absolutely poor if he or she is unable to purchase sufficient food to ensure 2,250 calories per day. (That, of course, allows nothing for clothing, housing, education, health services, etc.) If in India, one of the poorest countries in the world, it takes $50 per year to purchase minimum food supply, $50 of income is the standard for absolute poverty. Depending on purchasing power in other countries, that amount may vary—but the level of life will not.

One half of the 800 million absolutely poor live in south Asia (India, Pakistan, Bangladesh); one sixth live in east and southeast Asia (mainly Indonesia); one sixth live in sub-Saharan Africa; and the rest (100,000,000) are divided between Latin America, north Africa, and the middle east (35).

What is life like for these people? If you were a member of this destitute group you would most likely be illiterate (600 million adults in developing countries are illiterate; in addition, one third of primary school age children—one half of females—are not in school [33]). You would most likely be a landless laborer in a rural area, unreachable by decent roads, and out of the line of vision of most of the world. No doubt your parents and grandparents would

41

have been equally poor. You would work long hours, although malnourishment would probably dim the productivity of those hours. Four fifths of your earnings would go for food, and, at that, your diet would be one of the most bland and least satisfying of any in the world. (In India in 1973–74, 83 percent of household earnings for a typically poor family went for food, which only supplied an average of 1,500 calories per person [61].) You might well spend six hours a day simply obtaining water clean enough to wash and prepare food. Your life expectancy would be at least twenty-four years less than that of someone living in an industrialized nation.

As a random member of the absolutely poor, you might well be a child. (Two out of five of the absolutely poor are under ten.) You would watch many of your brothers and sisters die. (Of every ten children born to families in absolute poverty, two die within a year, another by age five; only five live to age forty.) Your physical and mental development would most likely be impaired by malnourishment, and your resistance to simple diseases such as measles, diarrhea and infection of cuts and scratches would be low. You would not go to school, and if you did go for one or two years, you might be too listless and apathetic from malnutrition and debilitating disease to learn. What is even worse, your potential to learn might have been permanently impaired by malnutrition in the first few months of your life.

You would live in a country where there is a high degree of inequality between the rich and the poor. You might well be a member of a minority group (a Latin American Indian or a member of a low caste in India). Above all else, your life would be extremely vulnerable. Your family might be prosperous enough one year to eat relatively well and perhaps to purchase some agricultural implements. The next year might be followed by drought, high food prices, and illness. No social services would help you through this period. The high level of insecurity in your life would make you afraid of risk; it might even make you afraid to adapt to policies that can help you.

Wordsworth notwithstanding, there is nothing romantic about this type of poverty, or its lesser forms. What may be the most shocking realization of all, however, is that absolute poverty and its deprivations are entirely unnecessary. Food supply in the world exceeds population. Many widespread diseases are preventible through efficiently administered vaccination programs. (Recent efforts in Nicaragua to combat malaria are paying off.) There is sufficient land to provide housing for those migrating to cities and farms for those remaining in rural areas. There is sufficient technology to supply clean water systems and sanitation systems for the present world population. Yet, 800 million persons continue to live in conditions that none of us, even those most dedicated to the simple lifestyle, would ever willingly choose.

The rest of this chapter will explore the physical aspects and causes of poverty. The next three chapters will examine other causes and influences.

Climate/Geography

Most poor countries are in the tropics (the area 23 degrees and 27 minutes on either side of the equator), especially in the regions of Asia and Africa. Why is that? Colonization has something to do with the locations of absolute poverty (see Chapter Four), but so does climate. Water-logged soil and dry soil are equally troublesome for agriculture. Waste disposal is more difficult in hot climates which promote bacterial growth. Water supply is becoming increasingly difficult in dry zones. Certain diseases flourish in the tropics (malaria, dysentery, and leprosy) because conditions for their multiplication are ideal.

Yet as definitive causes of poverty, climate and geography are not as important as they were once thought to be. No doubt, such factors as floods, droughts, supply of natural resources, and geography-specific diseases influence the level of life. Still, natural factors are less causal of famine and death than human factors such as food distribution, fluctuation of food prices, and inefficient farming methods. Let's look at how some of these natural and human factors reinforce one another.

Problems of Tropical Agriculture (Erosion, Deforestation)

The tropical climate is characterized by a relatively uniform temperature and uniform level of sunlight year round. Therefore, there is a year-round growing season. That is the good news. The bad news is that fragile tropical soils have a low nutrient content and are highly susceptible to erosion. Natural erosion is intensified by planting and irrigation practices, over-grazing, deforestation and other non-climatic factors.

In Guatemala, the rivers sometimes run brown from eroded soil. In Haiti, some slopes have eroded down to bedrock. In India, erosion rates are three times higher than in the United States. Eroded lands suffer increased loss of nutrients, are deficient in organic matter, are defenseless against environmental extremes, and are difficult to irrigate.

Irrigation, either to drain water-logged fields or to supply water to dry fields, is a continual problem for farmers in the tropics. Several problems caused by irrigation systems are the creation of insect breeding grounds in drained river basins and salinization of the soil. There is a strong need for careful planning of such systems.

Another problem area for tropical agriculture is deforestation. When lands are cleared for agricultural development and for domestic fuel, soil erosion increases as does the rate of water run-off, causing floods. (In 1973 Pakistan lost two million hectares of crops in low lying areas by such flood waters; 10,000 villages were wiped out [Lee 102].) In arid, semi-arid and subhumid areas in Africa, Asia, and Latin America, deforestation causes a decline in the productivity of land known as desertification. Developed nations are partially responsible for deforestation in tropical regions because the demand for tropical lumber in the first world has been steadily increasing. The prices exporters pay are often too low to cover replacement costs.

Reforestation can be eased through agro-forestry—combining forest and agricultural production, or growing forage for livestock underneath trees. Once again, there is a need for careful planning to overcome both ignorance and greed.

Famine

Famine can be defined as a "sudden collapse of the level of food consumption" (Sen 41). It *seems* to be caused by natural disasters such as drought and flood. The Bengal famine of 1943 followed a cyclone in October of 1942, torrential rains, and fungus disease. The Ethiopian famine of 1972–74 followed a period of erratic rains and drought. The 1974 famine in Bangladesh followed severe floods. All of these natural disasters are documented, and one would have to be a fool to discount them. But the fact remains that, in each case, if available food had been divided equally, mass starvation could have been prevented.

Bad weather certainly precipitated bad situations in these instances, but rocketing food prices, tardy response of governments and international organizations, and inefficient means of distributing available food turned bad situations into tragedy (*Poverty and Famines* 1982).

Energy/Natural Resources

Energy relates to natural resources, and to industrialization. Industrialized nations use eight times as much energy per person as middle-income nations and forty times as much as low-income nations, not only because they are industrialized, but also because households are more energy-intensive. Households in non-industrialized nations use non-commercial fuels (e.g. wood, dung) because they cannot afford commercial fuels. This has several drawbacks. The collection of fuel takes a great deal of time (five to nineteen work days per month for households in upland Nepal); gatherers are often children who ought to be in school; wood use depletes forests; and the burning of dung steals fertilizer from the soil and causes health problems. Exploration of alternate fuel sources in developing nations is both expensive and contributes little to the habits of the poor. Meanwhile, commercial fuel is exported from petroleum producing countries and is a major part of the import bill for most other developing countries.

Suffice it to say, while geographical, geological, and climatic conditions determine some aspects of development, poor planning, greed, and failure to respond to emergency situations (both inside and outside of a country) determine the impact of these conditions on human communities.

Population/Fertility

Does overpopulation cause poverty or vice versa? Are people poor because they have too many children, or do they have large numbers of children in response to being poor? Whether or not there are definitive answers to these questions, the problematic relationship between poverty and population is obvious.

The Problem of Overpopulation

Since 1950 the number of people in the developing world has doubled. The *percentage* of persons in these countries living in absolute poverty has decreased but the total *number* has increased. While increased population has brought prosperity to some countries who needed laborers and had adequate resources (i.e. Argentina), it has strained other economies. Increased fertility increases the number of people who are young, dependent, and not productive; it overloads the labor force and lowers wages; it overloads educational systems and decreases development of human resources. Children in large families tend to suffer from stunted growth and have shorter life expectancies than children in small families. (In addition to other factors, mothers whose health suffers from malnutrition and continual pregnancies produce children with smaller birth weights and wean them earlier [*World Development Report, 1980* 40].)

Decline of Fertility

One of the first myths that needs to be dispelled in a discussion of overpopulation is that programs which lower the death rate contribute to population growth. A number of studies indicate that population actually declines with a declining death rate, although there is often a considerable time gap between effects. To understand why this is so, one must understand the connection between poverty and high fertility.

In poor families, children are perceived as a form of investment—short-term investment in that they work and contribute to the family income pool, long-term investment in that they will support the parents in old age. These factors, in conjunction

Trends in birth and death rates, 1775–2050

(births and deaths per 1,000 population)[a]

50 *Per 1,000 population*

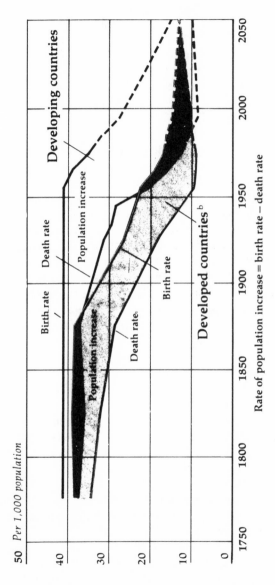

Rate of population increase = birth rate − death rate

a. Crude birth and death rates. The projected increases in death rates after about 1980 reflect the rising proportion of older people in the population.
b. Include industrialized countries, the USSR and Eastern Europe.

(*World Development Report, 1980* 64)

with the high rate of infant and child mortality in poor countries, encourages parents to have large families and to "overinsure" themselves. Moreover, when a child dies in infancy, the mother loses the natural contraceptive effect of breast feeding and may get pregnant again immediately.

Studies indicate, however, that if there are increases in family income and meaningful opportunities for female education and employment, along with a perceived pattern of lower infant mortality, the fertility rate will gradually decline. How? There are real barriers to family planning in developing countries. Contraceptive devices are often not available, and in many poor families give way to abstinence, clumsy illegal abortion, and infanticide. In addition, social and religious taboos make sex education difficult. Yet, studies of fertility indicate that culture is not an impenetrable barrier. Once a particular level of development has been reached, especially in the areas of education and employment opportunities for women, fertility rates fall through the "natural" means of delayed marriage age. (For example, in the 1960's the crude birth rate in South Korea and Peninsular Malaysia dropped half as much due to increased marriage age as to changes in marital fertility. Changes in the age of marriage proved to be *more* important than changes in marital fertility in Sri Lanka and the Philippines. [*World Development Report, 1980* 67])

Nonetheless, family planning is contributing to fertility control in a number of countries and in a number of ways. Clinics that provide sex education and contraceptives are increasing in number and effectiveness, especially in areas where women are encouraged to take charge of their lives. In China, tax and housing policies that discourage large families have worked. In Korea, two-child families receive free medical care and education if one parent is sterilized. In India, Bangladesh and Sri Lanka, persons who volunteer to be sterilized are compensated for their travel costs and work time. Other countries have raised the minimum age for marriage. (*World Development Report, 1984* 125–26)

Since 1965 the fertility rate in China, India and some other developing countries has declined by 10 percent. Continual increase in income for the poor and decline in mortality rates, plus increased education and job opportunities for women, can provide the context for even sharper decreases.

Basic Needs Shortfalls

One of the things that characterizes absolute poverty is the lack of certain basic resources that ensure a decent life—food, shelter, clean water, adequate sanitation, health care, education. In this next section we will look at these deprivations, what causes them and what they do to the quality of human life.

Shelter

What constitutes decent shelter is a relative question. Some climates require shelter that is well insulated and contains a source of heat; others do not. (After the recent earthquake in El Salvador, relief workers could construct emergency "chompas" very rapidly because of year-round moderate temperatures.) Shelter in urban areas is in more demand and needs to be more "intentional" than shelter in rural areas, where individual initiative is more appropriate.

The major problems in supplying decent housing for persons at the lowest end of the income scale are cost and availability of land. The two are related. "The poor do not live in crowded and unsanitary shelter because of ignorance of the alternatives. . . . Consumption of shelter is low because its price is high, and its price is high because of the failure of the supply system" (Churchill 5). Supply is difficult, especially in urban areas, because of the unavailability of affordable land. Where urban areas have expanded into areas normally used for agricultural production, land tends to be owned and monopolized by a few landholders. Squatters on these lands have neither rights nor services. In areas where the land is available, legal systems are often so cumbersome that the cost of transferring titles is prohibitive. In countries where the state owns the land, programs of distribution are often confused and irregular.

Services are a large part of any housing project. Without clean water and effective sanitation, shelter is incomplete. Yet where services are provided to the poor they are often irregular. It is not odd to find 85–100 percent of the people in an area supplied with electricity, while only 10–15 percent are supplied with clean water. The success of any program for housing demands coordination of land tenure, public services, financing and employment opportunities. It also demands realism. It is technologically feasible to provide decent housing for persons at the lowest end of the income scale, but that might mean public standpipes, pit latrines, and houses made of "traditional" materials. Unfortunately, many of the designers of such programs have notions of success based on their own socio-economic groups, and produce housing that the target group cannot afford. (7) (Habitat for Humanity has a history of realistic, culturally appropriate housing projects. They are presently working on a design for building blocks that go together without mortar, thus saving money on a commodity that often has to be imported and allowing for rapid slum clearance.)

Migration of the poor to urban centers will continue into the future, so urban housing will be an increasing problem. But unless policies for shelter are tied to policies for increase of income, and creation of jobs, they will only solve symptoms.

Safe Water/Sanitation

Infant deaths and adult diseases in the developing world are often related to deficiencies in clean water supply and waste disposal. Although a person can survive on one or two liters of water a day, 20 to 50 liters are necessary for drinking, food preparation, personal hygiene, and sanitation. Obtaining this water can be quite a task for the absolutely poor. In many rural areas people must walk one to five miles to get clean water, and in urban centers long queues collect at the few safe standpipes. (In a CARE study it was found that in rural Kenya, female heads of households spent 50 percent of their work time collecting water; 17 percent was spent in food preparation, and 21 percent in income-producing activities. In the city of Douala in Cameroon, two standpipes served 50,000 persons. [*Water Supply* 12]) Boiling water is not an efficient solution to the safe water problem, in that the cost/unavailability of fuel is prohibitive.

Irrigation needs often preclude personal needs in poor rural areas. In 1967 irrigation accounted for 70 percent of human use of water. This water is not readily available for domestic needs in that it evaporates, is transpired by plants, or becomes salinated. Irrigation needs will double by the year 2000. Moreover, it is predicted that several nations in Asia and Africa will have exhausted their available water supplies by the year 2000. [See chart.]

Another water-related problem is pollution. River waters, downstream from the cities in many developing nations, are highly polluted from mills, tanneries, refineries, and slaughter houses. In addition, river basin development for irrigation and the generation of electricity has caused health problems (malaria, river blindness), has flooded valuable lands, and has displaced populations.

Most important to water needs is the need for adequate waste disposal. Without this, no water supply will remain pure. Appropriate technology is, of course, important in the solving of sanitation problems, but so is education. Unless the people understand what germs are and how they spread, there is no reason to train their children in hygiene or to practice safe means of human waste disposal.

Nutrition

In spite of the fact that our present output of grain *alone* could supply every man, woman and child on the globe with 3,000 calories and 65 grams of protein per day, malnutrition occurs in all developing countries and is persistent in low-income countries. Unless comprehensive strategies for indigenous agricultural development and equitable means of distribution are undertaken, there is little hope for substantive improvement. In Asia and Africa "the quantity of food available to the poorest groups of people will simply be insufficient to permit children to reach normal body weight and intelligence and to permit normal activity and good health in adults" (*Global 2000 Report* 17).

For a long time it was thought that malnutrition was caused by an imbalance between calories and protein. The more common

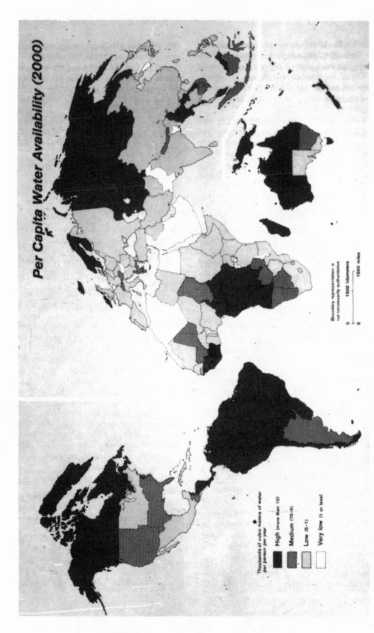

Per Capita Water Availability (2000)

(*The Global 2000 Report: Entering the Twenty-First Century* 25)

theory now is that it is caused by shortage of food intake, which is a direct reflection of poverty. People simply do not have sufficient income to afford food. (In 1959 it took 20 minutes of work in the United States to pay for one kilo of meat. The same kilo required 4.5 hours of work in Colombia. Five minutes of work in the U.S. would buy a liter of milk; the same liter would require 52 minutes in El Salvador. To purchase one kilo of meat, one kilo of bread, and one liter of milk, a person in El Salvador had to work for an entire day. [Belli 18]) The best continuing solutions for malnutrition are increases in income and purchasing power for households, and an increase in food production per person. Yet, once again, we enter the vicious cycle, for persons suffering from mulnutrition are weak, vulnerable to disease, and therefore less productive than the well-fed.

What are the consequences of protein-calorie malnutrition (PCM)? Common nutritional disorders in developing nations are nutritional anemia, endemic goiter, blindness due to vitamin A deficiency, other disorders due to vitamin deficiencies, and dental problems. Infection is more common in malnourished persons, especially children, due to the lowered effectiveness of the body's immune system. In addition, parasitic disease decreases nutritional intake through loss of appetite and intestinal malabsorption.

The most frightening effects of PCM, however, have to do with infant survival and with the physiological and mental development of children. To begin, the incidence of low birth weight (5.5 lb., or less) is excessive in rural and impoverished urban areas of low-income countries, and is directly related to the diet of the mother during pregnancy: ". . . improvement in nutritional status during pregnancy leads to a substantial decrease in incidence of low-birth-weight infants in pre-industrialized societies" (Lechtis 556). There are significant connections between low birth weight and infant mortality. If a child survives, he or she will probably stay with his or her birth weight category throughout the first eight years of his or her life (Mata 565). That is, a child with low birth weight will most likely remain underweight for these formative years.

If severe malnutrition accompanies weight retardation, which is often the case, the mental capacity of the child may well become permanently impaired. The first six months of life is the crucial time for development of intellectual potential. Severe PCM in these months seems to cause low levels of performance in adaptive behavior and therefore indicates a a probable loss of intellectual capacity (Cravioto and Robles 461).

Even discounting evidence of this nature, it is clear that inadequate nutrition is frequently associated with an inability to pay attention. Malnourished children cannot learn as effectively as well-fed children because they are listless, apathetic, weak, and are frequently absent from school because of illness. Since 60 percent of the total pre-school population of the world suffers from some degree of PCM, and since many malnourished children never even make it to school, this is quite an indictment for the future.

What would it take to reverse this trend? There is need for the following: (1) carefully administered food subsidies through coupons, or fair price shops, or price subsidies on foods consumed mainly by the poor; (2) targeted nutritional programs which supplement the diets of the most vulnerable; (3) fortification of common foods with iron, vitamin A, etc.; (4) growth monitoring and nutrition education; (5) effective agricultural programs which provide technical assistance, needed agricultural supplies, and credit to smallholder farmers; (6) land reform; (7) increased production of cheap sources of protein (beans and lentils); and (8) increased household income. Malnutrition cannot be considered in a vacuum; "poverty, disease and inadequate diets are intimately related and interwoven" (Caliendo 46).

In conclusion, there is both cause for hope and for despair. As Pedro Belli notes, "Practically every country in the world produces more calories and proteins than are needed to satisfy the needs of its population, yet protein-calorie malnutrition is probably the most common form of malnutrition" (18). Food production is expected to increase 90 percent in 1970–2000, yet food prices are expected to increase 95 percent in the same time period. This means that "the number of malnourished people in LDCs [less developed countries] could rise from 400–600 million in the mid-1970s to 1.3 billion in 2000" (*Global 2000 Report* 17). The bottom line appears to be this: If you can't afford to buy food, it doesn't exist for you.

Health Care

In low-income countries the life expectancy averages fifty years. Seventeen percent of people born will die before their fifth birthdays, as compared with 2 percent in industrialized countries. (In 1975 the deaths of children under five accounted for 48 percent of deaths in Brazil; in Sweden they account for 1 percent (*World Development Report, 1980* [54].) Common childhood diseases (diarrhea, measles) are many more times likely to kill children in developing countries than in prosperous countries. Why is this so? It is chiefly because of malnutrition and lack of vaccination. The scarcity of physicians in rural areas (60–70 percent of the doctors in developing countries reside in the cities where 20 percent of the population lives), lack of clean water supply, and low levels of health education also contribute substantially. In poor communities in general, debilitating diseases contribute to absenteeism from school, poor farm production, and a general sense of despair.

What is needed to reverse these debilitating trends? An increase in the purchasing power of households so that decent shelter, safe water, and medical supplies are affordable is mandatory. Also there needs to be improvement in the health of the environments in which poor people live. This would include heavy investment in public sanitation and in the control of communicable diseases through vaccination. The number of community health care workers and health care professionals in poor communities must increase, along with village clinics and referral hospitals. (In the mid-1970's in Bangladesh, there were 9,260 persons per physician, 5,600 persons per hospital bed, and 42,080 persons per nurse or midwife [57].) Finally, an increase in people's understanding of nutrition, disease, and hygiene must occur.

The World Health Organization and UNICEF are advocates of what they call "primary health care." It is an integrated approach to basic health care, including programs for improved nutrition, safe water/sanitation, health education, and vaccination. Primary health care promotes use of community health workers who do maternal and child health care, midwifery, family planning, and emergency care of injuries. In addition, these paramedical personnel work for immunization, safe water, and efficient waste disposal.

They do much of the health education in the community, including nutrition education. The recruitment, training and compensation of these health care workers, however, remains a problem.

Education

The dangers of shortfalls in this particular basic need have been mentioned so often in connection with other basic needs that only a summary is needed here.

Many studies have demonstrated the strong relationship between education and increased productivity. Thus, education appears to be a very attractive investment for developing countries, especially on the primary level. (The output of farmers who have completed four years of education is 13.2 percent higher than that of farmers without schooling [Noor 4].) In addition, there is a very strong relationship between literacy and increased life expectancy.

Still, school attendance in low-income countries is very low, and both teacher and student absenteeism is high. For each of the 315 persons presently enrolled in school in the developing world, three persons are not in school. In rural areas 40 percent drop out before their fourth year of primary education. (In 1974 in Brazil's poverty stricken northeast region, two thirds of the 46 percent enrolled in school dropped out before the second year. Only 4 percent of the starting group completed four years of school. [*World Development Report, 1980* 47].) As might be expected, a majority of the unschooled are female. This occurs in spite of the fact that primary school education of girls has statistically proven favorable effects on life expectancy, health, and fertility control.

In terms of health, studies in Bangladesh, Kenya and Colombia show that children are less likely to die if their mothers are educated. A study in Brazil indicated that children are more likely to be well fed if their mothers are educated. In both cases the improvement was without benefit of increase in income. In terms of fertility, education for girls increases chances for employment and delays the time of marriage. Women with a primary school education are also more likely to use contraceptives. Nonetheless, a strong bias against the education of women continues in many places.

In addition to measurable effects of education, one has to consider increase in the *capacity* for thinking and learning that comes with literacy and basic skills with numbers, as well as the receptivity to new ideas that can lead poor communities into visionary planning.

What is needed? Basic education is needed, education that is concentrated on the primary level and integrated with life needs. (In Nepal children have literacy classes in the morning followed by programs for work skills acquisition in the afternoon.) In addition, education needs to be designed for particular target groups—those who are least able to support themselves (landless farmers), those who are least able to speak for themselves (unprotected urban laborers), and those who have the highest potential for multiplying the effect of basic education (women, children). There is a need for curricular materials that are adapted to the linguistic and cultural backgrounds of students, for improved training of teachers, and for distance teaching such as educational radio programs that can reach a large number of persons. The rate of return on investments in education is so high in terms of increased human productivity that it should be given a very high priority by governments of developing nations and by international organizations.

Putting It All Together

It should be clear by now that absolute poverty results from an entangled web of physical and social factors. The incomes of the poor affect their health, educational level, nutrition and rate of reproduction. Educated parents are more likely to know about health, hygiene and nutrition; therefore, their children will probably die less often and be more alert. Improvements in nutrition may immediately increase fecundity, but its effects on education and income will in the long run decrease fertility.

Absolute poverty is not a tidy problem and it has no simple answers. But one thing that is sure is that it is *our* problem and that we must be about the business of seeking solutions. The fact that adequate natural resources and technology exist to provide basic needs to all persons makes absolute poverty a moral issue. We can choose to work toward a more just and caring redistribution of

Policy and poverty

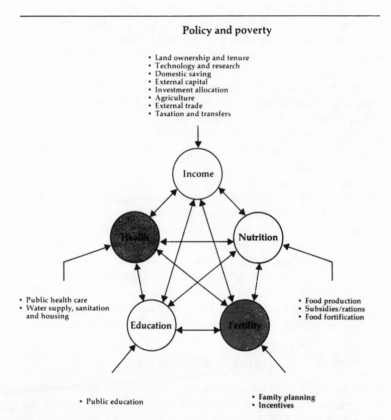

(*World Development Report, 1980* 69)

resources or we can, as individuals and nations, callously ignore its tragic dimensions. As Robert McNamara said in an address to the board of governors of the World Bank, "the attack on absolute poverty—basic human needs and their satisfaction—cannot be forever delayed, and cannot be finally denied by any global society that hopes tranquillity to endure." Perhaps, in light of Chapter One, we might add "justice and love" to "tranquillity."

BIBLIOGRAPHY

Ahluwalia, Montek, S., et al. "Growth and Poverty in Developing Countries," *Journal of Developmental Economics,* 6, (1979).

Belli, Pedro. "The Economic Implications of Malnutrition: The Dismal Science Revisited," *Economic Development and Cultural Change,* 20:1–23 (1971).

Caliendo, Mary Alice. *Nutrition and the World Food Crisis.* New York: Macmillan, 1979.

Cassen, Robert H. "Population and Development: A Survey," *World Development,* 4:10–11 (1976).

Churchill, Anthony and Margaret Lycette. *Shelter.* Poverty and Basic Needs Series. Washington, D.C.: World Bank, 1980.

Council on Environmental Quality and the Department of State. *The Global 2000 Report: Entering the Twenty-First Century,* vol. I. Washington, D.C.: U.S. Government Printing Office, 1980.

Cravioto, Joaquin and Beatriz Robles. "Evolution of Adaptive and Motor Behavior During Rehabilitation from Kwashiorkor," *American Journal of Orthopsychiatry,* 35:449–464 (1965).

Lechtis, Aaron, et al. "Maternal Nutrition and Fetal Growth in Developing Countries," *American Journal of Diseases of Children,* 129:553–561 (1975).

Lee, James A. *The Environment, Public Health, and Human Ecology.* Baltimore: Johns Hopkins University Press, 1985.

Mata, Leonard J., et al. "Survival and Physical Growth in Infancy and Early Childhood," *American Journal of Diseases of Children,* 129:561–566 (1975).

McNamara, Robert S. "Address to the Board of Governors," World Bank. Washington, D.C., September 26, 1977.

Noor, Abdun. "Education and Basic Human Needs," World Staff Working Paper, No. 450 (April 1981).

Sen, Amartya. *Poverty and Famines: An Essay on Entitlement and Deprivation.* Oxford: Oxford University Press, 1982.

World Bank. *Water Supply and Waste Disposal,* Poverty and Basic Needs Series. September 1980.

World Bank. *World Development Report, 1980.* New York: Oxford University Press, 1980.

World Bank. *World Development Report, 1984.* New York: Oxford University Press, 1984.

SUGGESTIONS FOR FURTHER STUDY

The Hunger Project. *Ending Hunger: An Idea Whose Time Has Come.* New York: Praeger, 1985.

Lappe, Frances Moore and Joseph Collins. *World Hunger: Twelve Myths.* New York: Grove Press, 1986.

Schumacher, E.F. *Small is Beautiful: Economics As If People Mattered.* New York: Harper and Row, 1973.

Sen, Amartya. *Poverty and Famines: An Essay on Entitlement and Deprivation.* Oxford: Calendon Press, 1982.

Streeten, Paul. *First Things First: Meeting Basic Needs in Developing Countries.* New York: Oxford University Press, 1981.

DISCUSSION QUESTIONS AND ACTIVITIES

1. The material in this chapter is disturbing. Take some time to express your reactions to the material. The response journals may help here. Try not to edit your responses at this point; be as open and spontaneous as possible.

2. Focus a bit on what it would mean to be absolutely poor. Consider your families and the styles of life to which they have become accustomed. Then list the things that they would have to give up in order to fit into the profile outlined in the first part of the chapter. Have someone record these things on a blackboard, or a sheet of newsprint, so that you have a collective record of "deprivations."

3. If you know of someone who grew up in a low-income country, invite that person to your meeting to tell what he or she has seen and experienced there.

4. For a day or two before you meet to discuss this chapter, keep a log of how many times you turn on the water, flush the toilet, open the refrigerator to fix a snack or meal, turn on the electricity, open a book or journal, or use an energy-supplied appliance. Also keep a record of the calories you consume and the

kinds of foods that supply these calories. Compare your lists by way of becoming conscious of how unconscious we are of our basic needs.

5. By way of personalizing all of this, discuss what you would do for a child from a low-income country should that child be miraculously placed on your doorstep.

6. Read over your response journals and raise issues that have not yet been discussed.

4

Recent History—Colonialism

This is Rudyard Kipling's call to the United States to join England in the colonial effort (1898):

Take up the White Man's Burden—
Send forth the best ye breed—
Go bind your sons to exile
To serve your captive's need;
To wait in heavy harness
On fluttered folks and wild—
Your new caught sullen peoples,
Half devil and half child.
from "The White Man's Burden"

Now compare George Orwell's response to being "forced" to kill a seemingly mad elephant while functioning as a colonial officer in Burma:

And it was at this moment, as I stood there with the rifle in my hands, that I first grasped the hollowness, the futility of the white man's dominion in the East. Here was I, the white man with his gun, standing in front of the unarmed native crowd—seemingly the actor of the piece; but in reality I was only an absurd puppet pushed to and fro by the will of the yellow faces behind. I perceived in this moment that when the white man turns tyrant it is his own freedom that he destroys. He becomes a sort of hollow, posing dummy, the conventionalized figure of a sahib. For it is the condition of his rule that he shall spend his life in trying to impress the "natives," and so in every crisis he has got to do what the "natives" expect of him.

He wears a mask, and his face grows to fit it. I had got to shoot the elephant. I had committed myself to doing it when I sent for the rifle. A sahib has got to act like a sahib; he has got to appear resolute, to know his own mind and to do definite things. To come all that way, rifle in hand, with two thousand people marching at my heels, and then to trail feebly away, having done nothing—no, that was impossible. The crowd would laugh at me. And my whole life, every white man's life in the East, was one long struggle not to be laughed at.

from "Shooting an Elephant"

One is tempted to compare colonialism with George Orwell's elephant—it was huge, cumbersome, slightly mad, dead on its feet, yet not without value, at least to our understanding. Colonialism is credited with changing the world geographically, politically, and economically. It is seen, in restrospect, as a blot on the moral development of western civilization. Theorists have spent long hours assessing and reassessing its motives and outcomes. Some see it as defensible error, some as self-perpetuating evil, and others as an amoral inevitability. Let's begin our discussion by looking at definitions, motives, and evaluative slants.

Definitions/Philosophy/Evaluations

What Is Colonialism?

As with many attempts at definition, we can begin with what colonialism isn't. It isn't *settlement*, the attempt by Europeans (sixteenth through eighteenth centuries) to establish societies like the ones they left behind in areas where the indigenous population was either sparse or easily controlled (i.e. British settlement in Australia and New Zealand). In these cases there may have been tensions between settled areas and mother countries and accusations of paternalism, but, in general, the relationship was not degrading. The settlement was a direct extension of European values and culture; quarrels were "in house."

The way that indigenous peoples were treated by the settlers (i.e. North American Indians by the English; South African blacks by the Dutch) comes closer to *colonialism* as it was experienced by Africa, Asia and the Pacific islands from 1870 to 1945.

Colonialism, as just described, was "the state of subjection—political, economic, and intellectual—of a non-European society [by a European society] which was the product of imperialism" (Fieldhouse 6). The colonials were alien and remained so. Emissaries came to the colony for "tours of duty," but sent money home, and returned to Europe for retirement. There was "no necessary identity of interest between rulers and ruled" (6). Inhabited territories were controlled by external political systems and interests. [See map of colonial possessions in 1914.]

Neo-colonialism, a term which came into use in the 1950's, describes the economic dependencies and exploitations that have persisted since colonial territories were nationalized (primarily after World War II) and which indicate that patterns set during the colonial period will be very hard to break. Analysts who use the term claim that colonialism impoverished the controlled territories through extraction of natural resources, promotion of cash crops (to the detriment of subsistence crops), and keeping the means of production and exchange in the hands of foreigners who were more likely to take profit out of the colony than to reinvest it. In the eyes of these analysts, colonialism created a pathological, self-perpetuating condition of "underdevelopment" in Asia and Africa which has not changed with decolonization, and industrialized nations have done little to break a pattern which serves them.

What Motivated Colonialism?

Political scientist Hedley Bull has speculated that before the concept of international society became intentional in the nineteenth century, relationships between "Christian" and "pagan" peoples were determined by a kind of "natural law"—all persons were conceived to be moral beings, but cultures differed widely in "fitness." Exploitation and enslavement took place in a such a hierarchy (one determined by cultural sophistication), but this had little to do with statehood and state relations as we now know them.

A more defined concept of international society came about when European states and independent political communities began to discuss common interests and outline rules to govern the fulfillment of these interests. Along with this came the recognition that states only have sovereignty when other states recognize the fact. This gave great power to those "setting up the rules." Thus, the European society of states became the world model, and "non-European states entered an originally European club of states as and when they measured up to criteria of admission laid down by the founder members" (123).

This set the stage for the "exportation" of western civilization in a simultaneously altruistic and exploitive fashion. Empires were in the making.

A collection of reasons why European powers took colonies in the nineteenth century would include: (1) a desire for strategic military strongholds; (2) a desire for bargaining chips in international relations; (3) national pride; (4) security for trade and investments; (5) a desire to raise revenue through taxes; and last, but never least, (6) a "civilizing mission" (Fieldhouse). This last motive is particularly interesting and complex, because although European powers saw themselves carrying "enlightenment" and godliness to benighted shores, they could not afford to bring the controlled population "up" to their level if they wanted to stay in power there. The fact that they did educate certain indigenous elites into the ruling bureaucracy was one of the subsequent causes of decolonization.

After World War I, when dependent territories were divided up as "protectorates" and "mandates," the concept of "sacred trust" entered the picture. It was an "act of humanity" for Britain to assume control of troubled Palestine. In addition, during the first part of the twentieth century, the discovery and often romanticizing of "primitivism" in art and social science affected motives for empire. African masks, brought to Europe, inspired painters such as Picasso to invent ways of depicting the instinctual and unconscious forces behind the cultivated appearance of reality. According to anthropologist Levy-Bruehl, the traditional people in Asia, Africa, and other sites were *pre*-logical, operating by mysticism rather than causality. They were intriguing to study but perceived as being bound to flounder in a world of complex economic

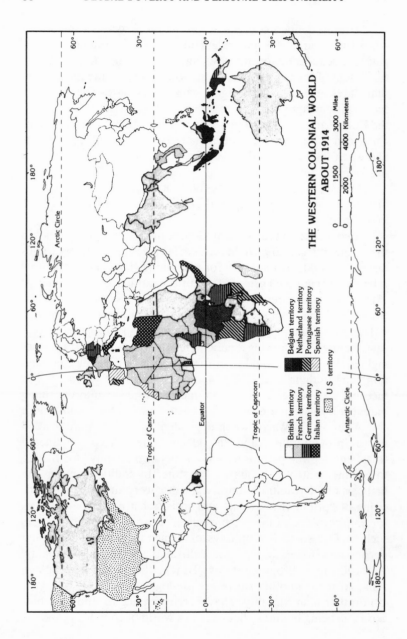

THE WESTERN COLONIAL WORLD
ABOUT 1914

British territory
French territory
German territory
Italian territory

Belgian territory
Netherland territory
Portuguese territory
Spanish territory

U S territory

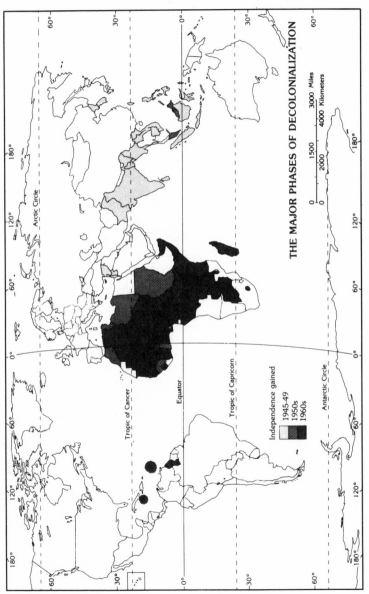

THE MAJOR PHASES OF DECOLONIALIZATION

Independence gained

1945-49
1950s
1960s

0   1500   3000 Miles

0   2000   4000 Kilometers

(Betts xviii–xix)

relationships. So, to the blatant economic needs on the part of post-World War I European powers for raw materials, extension of markets, and new places of investment was added a sense of paternal responsibility for these fascinating children of pre-industrial cultures.

How Is Colonialism To Be Evaluated?

The two quotes that head this chapter, both written by British "men of letters," indicate some of the breadth of opinion on the subject of colonialism, from within the system itself. In the late nineteenth century, a large literate public hungered for romances of exploration. Descriptive accounts of colonial territories by travelers, missionaries, soldiers, and officials were eagerly received. More critical accounts came from journalists and economists. After World War I, professional colonial administrators and scholars entered the publications scene with ponderous analyses. After World War II, historians were prominent, searching for indigenous source materials and predicting outcomes. The criticism of colonialism by economists and political scientists in this period became overtly polemical:

> To Marxists imperialism, colonialism and neo-colonialism all express the changing character of the hegemony exercised by the capitalist West over the rest of the world. To non-Marxists imperialism and its consequences may indicate a reluctant response to otherwise insoluble global problems or the pursuit of specific objectives of various kinds. (Fieldhouse 4)

Some of the most heated criticisms, as one might imagine, came from scholars of color, who saw patterns of racism at the very center of the colonial march toward empire and who saw the effects of colonialism as going much deeper than national boundaries and economic dependency. To Franz Fanon (*The Wretched of the Earth*) colonialism deprived peoples of the third world of their culture and their independent character, leaving them intellectually and morally disoriented. What he is describing here are the results of the "colonial mentality" whereby indigenous peoples were brought to accept their inferior status and to seek protection from alien powers.

At best, colonialism is seen as a complex improvisation to solve problems that at first seemed simple. This view holds that empire was an *outcome* rather than a motive of political/economic relationships between European states and southern territories. But however innocent its original motives, however inevitable empire might be as an historical phenomenon, nineteenth century colonization left behind a state of affairs that relates closely to the situation in developing countries described in Chapter Three:

> . . . the colonists exploited their dependencies, taking out more wealth than they created and, in the end, creating "underdevelopment," a condition in which all the mainsprings of economic and social development were cauterized because the imperial powers, or their nationals, came to control all the sources of wealth and applied them to their own ends rather than to the development of the colonies. (Fieldhouse 45)

An Historical Perspective on Colonialism

Geographical Aspects

National states in the third world, as we know them, did not exist before colonization. In fact, one might say that colonization "made" them. For example, Ghana is "an adopted name for an area with no natural, political or ethnic unity which was put together as a single colony, the Gold Coast, by the British during the late 19th century" (Fieldhouse 13). So when the population of the Gold Coast backed Kwame Nkrumah's campaign for independent statehood in the 1940's and 1950's, it was not to liberate an ancient kingdom, but a colonial amalgam. Such situations created internal problems for the independence movements. Often colonies were "convenient" collections of divergent ethnic, religious and social units which made unified statehood quite difficult. Significantly, the separation of Pakistan(s) from India, with all of its attendant violence, occurred on the very threshold of independence. Many years later, in 1971, civil war between East and West Pakistan continued that ethnic conflict. Thus some of the newly independent Asian and African nations are still struggling for internal unity, while simultaneously trying to find their place in the global economic order, and losing ground on both fronts.

Another geographical effect of colonialism was the creation of cities. As urban centers were formed and grew in the colonies, the slum problem increased as well. This meant that the dangers of fire and infectious disease (smallpox, malaria, typhoid, even bubonic plague) also increased. Europeans panicked. Therefore, an attempt to plan cities so that rulers and ruled lived separately seemed to be a conscious medical mandate as well as an assumed social mandate. In cities of the Belgian Congo, "indigenous quarters" were some 500 meters from European quarters—and, of course, more squalid and demeaning (Beris 180). The inequity that resulted was obscured, in part, by the "nativist" bias of anthropologists. Radical racial and economic segregation was explained in terms of cultural affinities. But as we all know, a ghetto is a ghetto—fertile ground for disease, illiteracy, overcrowding, discontent, and political isolation.

Economic Aspects

The immediate effect of colonialism on controlled territories is difficult to assess because so little is factually known about the pre-colonial conditions of these areas of the world. We are now living with the long-term effects of colonialism, which have already been alluded to.

But how were the colonies actually set up to benefit the mother countries? According to the British Navigation Acts of the seventeenth century, colonial trade took place on British ships; all imported goods came from Britain or arrived on British ships; all exports were transported to British ports, even if they were later shipped elsewhere; certain goods were forbidden to indigenous manufacturers; and the whole system was buttressed by tariffs. In the nineteenth century Britain became a "free trading" power, but a number of protective trade practices, chiefly tariffs, lingered in British and other European colonies.

European powers encouraged agriculture in their colonies, rather than industry, reasoning that colonies should be complementary rather than competitive with the metropolis. This usually meant the encouragement of cash crops for export. In India and Java, the production of sugar, jute, cotton, and tobacco for foreign consumption was encouraged, at least in part, by the imposition of taxes on farmers which forced them to sell their produce to generate cash. The same method was used in West Africa to stimulate production of palm oil and ground nuts. Cash crops provided agricultural variety and money to pay taxes and to purchase imports, but markets were uncertain and subsistence agriculture (the *basis* of survival) decreased. Some cash crops, new to the areas, "worked against themselves" economically in that they required special equipment for production which had to be imported at considerable cost, and in that they encouraged foreign-owned plantations which lowered labor motivation/production and increased managerial headaches.

The profit motive behind encouragement of cash crops led to a number of other methods to force the indigenous population to *work for the market.* Signed indentures, forced recruitment of labor for plantations, and "redistribution" of labor were common practices. Indian laborers were moved to Malaya, Burma, Ceylon, and central and southern Africa; Chinese laborers were moved from Hong Kong to southeast Asia and other places. [See chart.] The sociological problems incurred by forced migration of labor are obvious. Peasants were physically dislocated, culturally disoriented, and often separated from the products of their own labor.

Colonial powers did not encourage industrialization in their possessions until after 1945. Then production tended to go in two directions: the processing of primary products (food, natural resources) for export and the manufacture of items for the domestic market, thus avoiding competition with colonial powers in the global market.

Dispensation of Chinese Population Due to Labor Relocation During Colonial Rule (Figures from 1931)	
BURMA	194,000
INDOCHINA	418,000
INDONESIA	1,233,000
PHILIPPINES	72,000
MADAGASCAR	2,500
JAMAICA	4,000
	(Betts 106)

Political Aspects

The governance of the colonies, either by direct alien administration, or by indirect rule (the incorporation of chieftains and provincial councils), is almost everywhere described as bureaucratic. Decisions were not made by parliaments and prime ministers back home but by civil servants and agencies of a variety of sorts, protecting the interests of the parent states, of course.

Technically, there were three types of colonial possessions: imperial possessions, protectorates, and mandates. In the case of "imperial possessions," international law levied no limitation on sovereignty of parent states, and subjected peoples had no nationality other than that of European possessions. "Protectorates" were dependent territories attached to a parent state by treaty, usually providing protection from a third power. "Mandates" were conquered territories dispersed by international agreements and usually promised independence at a prescribed time.

The "protectorate" and "mandate" phenomena were particularly important to the balance of powers between the world wars and after World War II when "keeping the world safe for democracy" was often cited as a motive for control of dependent territories. But the lines of demarcation between "imperial possessions," "protectorates," and "mandates" were not clearly maintained, particularly in pre-United Nations days, and countries in the latter two categories, at times, slipped into the former (i.e. British and German East Africa, Nyasaland, and Cameroons).

The most interesting political aspects of colonialism occurred during the period of decolonization and will be discussed further in the next section.

Decolonization and Its Aftermath

Attempts at Reform

After World War I, a number of factors conspired against empire building. Population growth created problems which called into question the ability of colonial governments to handle indigenous problems: "The bureaucracy was well aware by the 1930s that the test of colonial government lay in boosting food supply so that rising population could be turned into an asset, not a liability" (Holland 4). In addition, their attempts to educate the indigenous middle class came back to haunt European states. Native elites, in frustration over economic stagnation and fear of slipping back into destitution, began to support movements toward national independence. (The educated middle class in India was a definite force behind Gandhian protest.) Indigenous religious groups (Buddhists in Burma, Muslims in the Netherlands Indies), in fear of absorption and/or repression, began to move toward nationalism. The great depression caused a dislocation between industrial and agricultural prices which worked against cash crop economies. The "depression had suddenly knocked away the supports which had made colonials so acceptable to the generation of their parents," and students began to riot (12). In the wake of the depression, some larger colonies (India, the French and Dutch empires) moved toward industrial development, therefore toward political and social maturation (as defined by colonial powers), therefore toward independence.

If colonial powers wanted to remain "in the game," they needed to change direction substantially. In 1929 the British parliament passed the Colonial Development Act which was designed to aid industry and agriculture within the colonies and to aid commerce with the United Kingdom. Education for "useful-ness" in technical schools prepared more "natives" to be "wage earners." Meanwhile literacy training in English was increased for indigenous elites who by this token found their way into the "system."

In 1935 Britain passed the Government of India Act which created an all-India federation and provided for provincial self-government which clustered minorities. This act both recognized the minorities as substantial units and kept them precariously bal-anced against one another. Meanwhile, Britain used commercial and diplomatic constraints on economic and political diversifica-tion. If this sounds circular, it was. What was given with one hand was controlled by another in a very skillful attempt to "keep the lid on." In African colonies, indirect rule was used to set up cadres of nationals who were all too willing to exploit the powers that their privileged closeness to the British gave them.

Decolonization came quickly and sometimes violently, both because of and in spite of conciliatory efforts on the part of Euro-pean powers.

Decolonization

For the United States World War II was an opportunity to crack the European empires and gain access to new areas of the world. Understandably, after the war the U.S. took an anti-colonial position, supported the self-determination of nations, and pressed for open markets. This, plus ideological pressures at home, caused Britain and other European countries to begin to let go of their territories. Indigenous national movements and threats of resulting guerrilla war did their parts to encourage such a move. But the crowning motivation, as always, was economic. The colo-nies were simply becoming too expensive. In the late 1940s and early 1950s, it was naively assumed that large amounts of develop-ment aid alone would cause poor economies to become self-generating: "Technology and economic aid were exported in large quantities during the final days of colonialism. But they were miniscule in relation to the need for meaningful development . . ." (Betts 199). Therefore, in some cases, colonies were "hustled toward independence" in order to release European funds for home use.

In short, while there were seventy-one sovereign states before World War II, now there are over one hundred and sixty, many of them suffering from political confusion and dangerously vulnerable economic systems.

Neocolonialism

Both the subject of economic development and the process of development as observed in the Third World are products of a changing world—of the aftermath of the Second World War, of the end of empire and of the spread of nationalism to the far corners of the earth. (Griffin 221)

Keith Griffin is here expressing a generally accepted perception. But one is tempted to ask if the end of empire (decolonization) changed the world all that much. Empire necessitated that "the pattern of production and trade, the way in which investable resources were appropriated and allocated, and the development of human resources through education and training were all largely determined externally to the societies concerned" (221). In many eyes, decolonization was a shift, perhaps even a tightening, rather than a radical change in this pattern of dependency.

New nations who wanted to enter the world market entered a market clearly determined by European needs and values. And there were obstacles to their full entry, at home and abroad. At home, European-trained, bureaucratic elites (sometimes called the comprador class) used their power to monopolize financial surpluses, usually from cash crop farming. Abroad there was little encouragement. European powers had their own problems and disengaged themselves from third world needs—needs not for "petty aid patronage" but for a restructuring of world market patterns. (R.F. Holland claims that "what the Falklands highlighted was a Britain which cared very little about what Africans, Asians or the rest of Latin America thought on an issue where British interests were held to be at stake" [292].)

As always, the economic situation did not remain static; things have gotten worse. Post-decolonization changes in technology and industry have greatly widened the gap between have and have-not nations and supplied "advanced" means of exploitation of the have-nots (i.e. wholesale movement of raw materials from non-industrial to industrialized nations; radical imbalances between imports and exports).

And the gap is not simply between third and first world nations. Since decolonization, the difference between incomes per head *within* third world countries has increased faster than that *between* third world and first world nations, in addition to the fact that richer developing countries have grown faster than poorer developing countries, which means that some of the most needy nations (i.e. Bangladesh, Chad, Niger) "are absolutely worse off than they were two decades ago" (Griffin 222).

Can all of this really be blamed on colonization and its lingering patterns of dependency? Analysts of the left say, "Absolutely!" The only true independence for third world countries would be to reject transnational additional capitalism, nationalize foreign-owned assets, throw off foreign debt, and attack poverty through radical redistribution of wealth, culturally appropriate education, land reform, and labor-intensive indigenous industry. Other analysts cite wider political causes for present economic inequities (i.e. superpower geopolitical competition, corruption within third world states, ill-conceived domestic price policies, and poor administration of foreign and domestic investment and development assistance), yet still call for a strong emphasis on national self-reliance and the development of indigenous human resources.

In conclusion, whether colonial powers underdeveloped the third world or merely left it vulnerable to underdevelopment is almost irrelevant. The fact remains that the increasing gap between prosperous and developing countries is cause for grave concern. It is also true that prosperous nations, whether by choice or by legacy, continue to "call the shots" in global economics. The real question, then, is how the vicious circle of debilitating dependencies can be broken, how dependents can become respected co-equals, managing their own development and participating freely in the world market. Chapter Five will take a closer look at this process.

BIBLIOGRAPHY

Betts, Raymond F. *Uncertain Dimensions: Western Overseas Empire in the Twentieth Century.* Minneapolis: University of Minnesota Press, 1985.

Bull, Hedley. "The Emergence of a Universal International Society," *The Expansion of International Society,* edited by Hedley Bull and Alan Watson. Oxford: Clarendon Press, 1984.

Fieldhouse, D.K. *Colonialism 1870–1945: An Introduction.* New York: St. Martin's Press, 1981.

Frank, Andre Gunder. *Crisis in the Third World.* New York: Holmes and Meier Publications, 1981.

Griffin, Keith. "Economic Development in an Changing World," *World Development,* 9:221–226 (1981).

Holland, R.F. *European Decolonization 1908–81: An Introductory Study.* New York: St. Martin's Press, 1985.

Kedourie, Elie. "A New International Disorder," *The Expansion of International Society.*

Loup, Jacques. *Can the Third World Survive?* Baltimore: Johns Hopkins University Press, 1980.

SUGGESTIONS FOR FURTHER STUDY

Evans, Peter. *Dependent Development: The Alliance of Multinationals, State, and Local Capital in Brazil.* Princeton: Princeton University Press, 1979.

Frank, Andre Gunder. *Crisis in the Third World.* New York: Holmes and Meier Publications, 1981.

Kierman, V.G. *The Lords of Human Kind: Black Man, Yellow Man, and White Man in an Age of Empire.* New York: Columbia University Press, 1986.

Loup, Jacques. *Can the Third World Survive?* Baltimore: Johns Hopkins University Press, 1980.

Memmi, Albert. *The Colonizer and the Colonized,* translated by Howard Greenfield. New York: Orion Press, 1965.

Myrdal, Gunnar. *Asian Drama: An Inquiry into the Poverty of Nations,* abridgement by Seth S. King. New York: Pantheon Books, 1972.

Orwell, George. "Shooting an Elephant," "A Hanging," from *Burma Days,* "Rudyard Kipling," "Reflections on Gandhi," *The Orwell Reader.* New York: Harcourt, Brace and Company, 1956.

DISCUSSION QUESTIONS AND ACTIVITIES

1. Colonialism cannot help but remind one of unhealthy parenting, parenting that involves over-direction, egocentrism, and enforced immaturity. Take some time to talk about parenting styles that are supportive, yet respectful of individual differences. Under what conditions does the child become the parent?

2. Think back to the time when you were breaking away from parental control. What attitudes did you resent on the part of your parents and why? How did you see yourselves in relationship to your parents? Encourage one another to do some personal story-telling; then apply your findings to the historical pattern described in Chapter Four.

3. The United States is more involved in neo-colonialism (the present economic dependency of third world nations on industrialized nations) than it was in the colonial/decolonial process per se. Reflect on this. How have North Americans "inherited" European views toward the third world and its peoples? How are these attitudes manifest in attitudes toward Latin America? Toward migrant workers?

4. Take a few minutes to think about what, for each one of you, represents a recent example of new-colonial thinking. It could be a world event, a foreign policy issue, a news slant, or a racial incident. Discuss your examples and speculate about possible "solutions" for each.

5. Take a look at your response journals and bring up pertinent issues raised there.

5

International Aspects of Poverty

The last chapter looked at some of the historical patterns that preceded and contributed to our present state of global economic disparity. This chapter will look at international aspects of poverty and its alleviation: dependency theory, the developing countries' call for a New International Economic Order (NIEO) and its implications for international relations, and, finally, the much debated issue of foreign aid.

Dependency Theory

According to economists who subscribe to dependency theory, the world consists of a developed center and of an underdeveloped periphery. Countries in the center (chiefly Europe, Japan, and North America) are technologically advanced and retain their economic advantages over the periphery through their influence on international trade. The periphery is thus dependent on the policy-making power of the center, and the center is dependent on the "strategic minerals, cheap labor, and markets of, principally, underdeveloped societies" (Munoz 2). The pattern of colonial economics is clearly analogous, and to some degree (depending on one's analytical stance) causal.

Dependency and Latin America

To get a clearer sense of how dependency evolves and works to the disadvantage of countries on the periphery, let us look at the impoverishment of Latin America. Latin America is an interesting area in that it falls somewhere between European settlement (i.e. the U.S., Australia, New Zealand) and European colonization (i.e. nineteenth century empire building). The Spanish and Portuguese "settled" there early on, simultaneously absorbing, enslaving, and indenturing the indigenous population, which remained very much in evidence nonetheless. Decolonization was not possible, any more that it is for South Africa, because the Europeans had moved in—in all ways. Yet Latin America never lost its non-European cultural orientation, and the region has clearly been treated as a conduit of raw materials for European and North American industries.

By the decade of the 1940's, nation-states in Latin America were having to come to grips with the results of "exploitation of a considerable part of their natural resources—land and minerals—as a result of the industrial countries' needs for food and raw materials" (Sunkel 93). These "results" included depletion of reserves of non-renewable resources, loss of tropical forests, and impoverishment of the best agricultural lands. For years, surplus capital had either flowed abroad or gone for the purchase of luxury items for rich landowners and urban elites.

After World War II, Latin American states began to take more control of their imports and exports. The industrial sector was moving toward heavy industry (iron, steel, cement, electricity) which provided the necessary inputs for domestic development and supplied reliable exports. But with the rising influence of multinational corporations (MNCs) in the late 1950's, the picture radically changed. Industry switched to capital-intensive and energy-intensive ventures (automobiles, consumer items) which relied heavily on the importation of raw materials (including oil), semi-manufactured products, technology, etc. Hence industry became more vulnerable to erratic shifts in the international market.

Simultaneously, the "green revolution" brought advances in agriculture which required new expenditures in fertilizers, seeds, and irrigation technology. Farming was more capital-intensive (less labor-intensive) than it had been, and migration to cities increased. This brought urban housing shortages, exploitive rents, squatter settlements, and a resultant increase in disease and squalor. In addition, the modernization of farming encouraged the clearing of forests (and subsequent desertification), the salination of water from irrigation systems, and the evolution of pesticide-resistant varieties of insects which increased the incidence of malaria.

Progress was being made in variety of exports and in agricultural technology, but at whose expense? And to whose gain? Having pulled its head "above water" in the 1940's, Latin America slipped back into a dependent situation when it could not "complete its economic cycle except by an exclusive (or limited) reliance on an external complement" (Munoz 48). That external complement was chiefly the U.S., base for a majority of MNCs, exporter of agricultural technology, and market for most Latin American exports. Analysts can argue all day about U.S. motives for involvement in Latin American economies; the dependent relationship is what needs to be addressed.

As Osvaldo Sunkel states, "Growth has to continue in Latin America in order to generate the means required for the satisfaction of the basic needs of the population, but it will have to be part of an alternative style of development" (109). That style should include an industrial change from fossil energy to more renewable, less polluting sources; more labor-intensive, resource-appropriate technologies; local management of business; and a plan for dealing with cities and media-inspired consumerism. All of this could lead to increased self-reliance for Latin American economies.

Evaluation of Dependency

Dependency, as defined by James Caporaso and Behroux Zare, is a structural condition—"the process by which less developed countries are incorporated into the global capitalist system" (44). This process of economic assimilation has seemed to be inevitable as a means to economic growth in developing countries; therefore, dependency has seemed to be inevitable. But not everyone agrees on its impact. Radical, leftist analysts see it as retarding growth; conservatives see it as positively related to growth; the centrists see it as a response to expansion at the center, i.e. in the industrialized nations. However one approaches this issue, the portrait of inequality is compelling. For example, the exportation of twelve primary commodities (including oil) accounts for 80 percent of the export earnings of developing countries. Final consumers pay $200 billion for these primary commodities, while the producers receive only $30 billion (15 percent). In addition, the purchasing power from these primary exports (e.g. cocoa, coffee, sugar, tin) in relation to imported manufactured goods continues to decline (ul Haq, "Negotiating a New Bargain with the Rich Countries" 119). Thus the least developed countries are in a progressively losing situation and are increasingly dependent on foreign assistance to achieve some balance of payments.

The present debt crisis faced by many third world countries is directly related to the issue of dependency. An interesting case study is sub-Sahara Africa where although the debt itself is relatively small, the cost of servicing the debt raises total indebtedness to 30–50 percent of the area's GNP (*World Development Report, 1986* 52). The problem for Africa and for other developing areas is whether economic growth can meet both debt obligations and the need for domestic investment. Several countries in Latin America have decided that it cannot and have, by refusal of interest payments, forced foreign banks to reschedule their loans.

Whatever has been the role of economic dependency in the past—destructive, supportive, or inevitable—it seems to have reached a point of insupportability. In response, the developing countries have put forth a call for a New International Economic Order, one that encourages self-reliance and economic dignity for southern nations. In developed countries, this call has stimulated an intense analysis of international relations and of the concept of global interdependence.

The Possibility of a New International Economic Order (NIEO)

The call for a NIEO came from the developing countries as a response to their disappointment with foreign aid, to the debt crisis, to balance of payment problems, to trade barriers restricting access to developed countries' markets, to their disappointment with the outcomes of political independence (neo-colonialism), and to the success of OPEC (Organization of Petroleum Exporting Countries) in bargaining with the first world. A contributing cause may have been the integration of ruling elites from third world countries into the prevailing world economic order, which has brought the dualism between haves and have-nots very close to home.

If taken seriously, this call would move the world powers to a recognition and encouragement of the self-reliance of developing countries (including increased collective bargaining power and the development of south-south trading relationships); a search for mutual interests between nations of the north and south; and the formulation of mutually acceptable rules and procedures for foreign trade. Thus, both respect for individual nations and interdependence would be encouraged.

State-Centric vs. Globalist Views

The debate over whether nationalism or interdependence is most important in foreign policy has been a heated one since the institutionalization of political science after World War I. The so-called realists argued that national power is a kind of "natural drive." Thus nationalism is inevitable, and only a sane balance of power can provide security. The idealists, on the other hand, argued that only a collective approach to the international order could provide peace and security. They called for the end of secret diplomacy and the establishment of a world governing body (at first, the League of Nations).

In recent times the debate has shifted. Now we speak of a state-centric view versus a globalist view. The state-centric view, as defined by Oran Young, postulates that "the state in its modern form is the fundamental political unit in the world system and that, therefore, it is possible to analyse world politics largely in terms of interstate relations" (Maghoori 14). According to this view, political and non-political activities are defined by reference to boundaries and state systems.

The globalist view, again according to Young, holds that "rapid and continuing developments in a variety of areas such as communications, transportation, and military technology have caused an effective shrinking of the world and have led to a situation in which the state, nation-state, and state system are increasingly obsolescent and ineffective structures for the achievement of human security and welfare" (16). In the eyes of these analysts, war has become dysfunctional as a means of diplomacy due to the awesome power of nuclear weapons, and international organizations (including MNCs) are on the rise. Therefore, global interdependence is the wave of the future.

To ardent globalists, interdependence among nations is not only the wave of the future—it is the hope of the future. As they argue, "the higher the level of interdependence in a world system, the harder it becomes to maintain qualitatively unequal relations among the units of the system" (Young 24). To reluctant or anti-globalists, this notion is naive and overlooks functional inequities for the sake of utopian dreams. In a system where 42.5 percent of Peru's 1966 exports and 18.2 percent of India's exports came to the U.S., yet only made up 1.2 percent of U.S. imports, mutual interdependence hardly defines the situation (Waltz 87). In spite of the favorable rhetoric of interdependence, these analysts argue, the fact remains that "where disparities are great, whether among firms or states, the largest of them need worry least about the bothersome activities of others" (Waltz 92).

The Demands of a NIEO on International Relations

What changes in international relations are necessary to bring about realistic global interdependence while still honoring the needs, rights, and values of sovereign states, many of whom, as discussed in the last chapter, are just discovering these things for themselves?

One strategy calls for an initial delinking of third world countries from first world, chiefly capitalistic interests. This is seen as necessary to the process of self-discovery and consolidation of interests. Using China as an example of successful self-development, Mahbub ul Haq argues that developing countries need to turn inward in order to develop consumption values that do not seek to emulate the (for them) impossible lifestyles of the rich. They need to examine economic systems impartially, without external coercion, and select the one that suits their needs. As ul Haq realistically asserts, capitalism, which dominates the present economic world order, will only work in situations where inequality of income can be tolerated for a long time and where governments are willing to be supported (and shaped) by western allies. For many developing countries, genuine, indigenous socialism (not an exported brand) may be the best short- or long-term system.

Delinking from the first world would entail designing anti-poverty strategies, forming alliances between students and peasants/workers, developing indigenous technology, paying attention to national history, and studying carefully the effects of multinational corporations on host states. According to ul Haq, this "retrenching" of individual third world nations should parallel the formation of a new international order that, according to his speculations, would need to include: (1) a World Development Authority (under the auspices of the United Nations) to regulate trade and global economic planning; (2) an International Central Bank with the ability to create international currency and to set up lines of credit to nations not based on previous affluence; and (3) a new framework for the transfer of resources from prosperous countries to developing countries that is more reliable and more grant-based than present foreign aid (*The Poverty Curtain*).

As Mahbub ul Haq, a Pakistani involved in economic planning for many years, points out, the failure to pull off a program of mutual respect and cooperation between the developing and developed worlds may very well result in confrontation. At our present rate of change in prosperity, by the middle of the next century the rich nations are going to have 10 percent of the world's population and control 70 percent of the world's income. The poor will be numerous enough to demand radical change, probably through violence. (Of the developing countries, India, Pakistan, and China already have nuclear capability, and one suspects that the list of countries capable of initiating nuclear destruction will increase steadily.) In the past, the rich and powerful have rarely willingly given up privileges for the good of others. Much, then, depends on how clearly *all* nations see the advantages of a new balance between economic self-determination and global mutuality.

South-South Cooperation

Between inward-looking isolationism and a massive restructuring of the global order stands the possibility of cooperation between southern nations. Since southern nations need to grow faster than northern nations, they may well need to delink from world trade *as an economic group*. This would mean general encouragement of agricultural production, emphasis on substituting domestic commodities for imports, and south-south trade. South-south trade could lead to a common fund for necessary price adjustments, the development of third world multinationals, and buyers' associations (Haq, "Beyond the Slogan of South-South Co-operation" 747). It could lead to increased dialogue among third world powers which could itself lead to intellectual liberation, increase in third world bargaining power, and the formation of a third world secretariat—all helping to bridge the gap between vulnerable individual states and global institutions.

Movement in the direction of a "new paradigm" for international relations that includes strong indigenous and collective elements is frightening for the old order because there are no pre-set, guaranteeable rules to govern its development. As a possible solution, Robert Rothstein proposes the guided evolution of overlapping sets of rules—rules for relations between developed countries, between developing countries, and between developed and developing countries. As he suggests, "separate systems with different but interlocking sets of rules may be more realistic than *global* rules" (272). Each set of guidelines would need to be contextual and realistic. For developing countries this would mean scaling down expectations for international systems, concentrating on domestic productivity, and taking collective (third world) self-reliance seriously. For developed countries this would mean working toward long-range, carefully researched policies that avoid the "quick fix" approach.

Morality as an Issue

As some analysts suggest, this evolution toward a NIEO might well entail modest amounts of sacrifice on the parts of prosperous nations—sacrifice in the correction of gross political inequalities and trade biases, in the transfer of resources from rich to poor nations, and in making room for the "voice" of developing countries in global negotiations (Streeten, "Approaches to a NIEO"

14). Discussion of sacrifice necessitates the introduction of humanitarian moral arguments into the academic/professional arena (already occurring in the articulation of Scandinavian aid policy). This may engender some resistance, for in the developed world, religion and ethics have become so privatized that what was a given in ancient Greece (a philosophical connection between ethics and politics) has here become a revolutionary idea. Yet, according to Paul Streeten, it is a necessary phenomenon:

> The principal reason why moral obligation must be accepted by governments (as well as individuals) is that certain objectives can be achieved only through collective action, such as indivisible projects, or stepping up growth rates by adding foreign savings in the form of aid, or intervention on behalf of children of poor households, a particularly vulnerable and particularly neglected group. ("Development Dichotomies" 878)

Hopefully, one day, individuals, lobby groups, and nations will be as concerned about their moral development as they are about their economic development, or at least recognize the connection between the two. Yet even in cases where compassion prevails, intelligence must plan. This brings us to the complex issue of foreign aid. How many of us have looked at surpluses of wheat in the developed world and said, "Why can't this be sent to the malnourished?" It can, but it just might destroy farmers' incomes and initiative in the process. The implementation of economic justice and transcultural love requires time, thought, sweat, and an ability to admit mistakes.

Foreign Aid

Definitions

Foreign aid is defined as a "transfer of resources on concessional terms—on terms, that is, more generous or 'softer' than loans obtainable in the world's capital markets" (Cassen 2). Assistance qualifies as "aid" if its main objectives are the promotion of

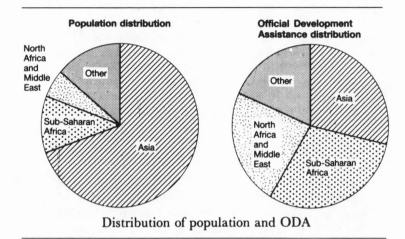

Distribution of population and ODA

(Cassen 3)

economic development and welfare, if it is proffered by official agencies (nations or multilateral organizations) and if it has a "grant element" of 25 percent or more. (This includes so-called soft loans—loans sufficiently below the market interest rate to meet the 25 percent grant factor.) Resources for military purposes are excluded; food aid and technological assistance are included.

What is aid used for? Traditionally it goes for infrastructure (i.e. transportation/communication systems), agricultural needs, manufacturing needs, basic human services (water, health care, education, etc.), skilled manpower, and the formation of administrative institutions. In the past, aid has been most successful in Asia, while the sub-Saharan African nations remain virtually untouched by its effects. This, of course, raises the question of whether aid *can* work in a situation where political structures are unstable, administrative institutions immature, the people chiefly illiterate, and the population growing by leaps and bounds.

Growth versus Poverty

There are three categories of recipients of aid: low income countries (i.e. countries with per capita incomes below $600, according to 1980 prices); lower-middle income countries, with per capita incomes from $600 to $1,200; and upper-middle income countries, whose per capita incomes are above $1,200 (Cassen 29). Most aid goes to lower income countries (which include India) and, increasingly, to a subgroup of this category, the *least* developed countries (many sub-Saharan African nations, Bangladesh, Haiti). Much of this aid goes to bolster government budgets (12 percent in India, 80 percent in Mali), which then support infrastructure, transportation, health care, education, etc. Aid is also used to bolster a country's balance of payments during transition periods when imports are likely to grow faster than exports. Some assistance is designated for particular development projects and some takes the form of material aid (food and supplies). In general, the returns on development assistance are very difficult to measure and ought *not* to be measured strictly in terms of GNP.

The question remains, then—if growth in GNP is an inappropriate measure of success, what measure is appropriate? Moreover, is the reduction of poverty a feasible goal? Aid can relieve poverty in several ways: (1) creating conditions for an increase in the incomes of poor households, (2) specific small-scale infrastructure projects, (3) supplying basic needs (education, health care, housing, family planning, etc.), (4) facilitating social change through education, and (5) assisting in policy reforms (45). The highest priority need for the rural poor is often food and water. Since the poor sometimes spends 75 percent of their income on food, a good aid strategy is to *subsidize* food stuffs primarily eaten by the poor. This will keep prices favorable for farmers yet make food affordable to consumers. When encouraging the *production* of food, donors can once again accomplish much by concentrating on foodstuffs consumed largely by the poor (millets, sorghum, cassava).

Other aid strategies to alleviate poverty include the building of food storage facilities, which uses local labor and encourages future planning; adjusting rural credit so that the poorest qualify for loans; and supporting labor-intensive public works. Primary health care and primary education have high rates of return in developing countries (as discussed in Chapter Three). Yet one of the most crucial areas of need in poor countries is land reform (both rural and urban). Aid can ease reform through compensation to landowners and through supply of materials to till "new" lands (farm equipment, seeds, fertilizers).

Factors that keep aid from helping the poorest are: failure to research the probable impact of aid (i.e. building a road to open up local production, only to have large-scale manufacturers come in and destroy local crafts); ignoring women's roles in alleviation of poverty (also discussed in Chapter Three); and haphazard administrative policies. Unfortunately, "most of the poorest countries have made little progress against poverty, often despite substantial aid" (49), but, as Robert Cassen is quick to add, who knows how bad the situation would be without foreign assistance?

Food Aid

Aid programs usually break down into project aid (money directed to a particular target group and/or activity), program aid (money directed to an entire economy and accompanied by policy negotiations), and food aid (usually program aid given in kind). Food aid is the most highly contested form of aid, often accused of being a less than charitable occasion for the U.S. to dump its agricultural surpluses which, in turn, depresses farm incomes and, at times, creates special tastes in a people that can only be met through subsequent export sales. The cynicism about motives most likely stems from the frequent lack of success or backfiring of systemic food aid. It should be emphasized, though, that food aid is quite often successful as relief or emergency aid.

The main problem with food aid is what it can do to prices. When the market is flooded by increased supply, prices fall. This is good for consumers, but bad for producers. Provision must be made, therefore, to maintain incentive prices for farmers. This can be accomplished through government subsidies or a well-orchestrated balance between supply and demand.

If the purpose of food aid is to provide supplementary nutrition for the most vulnerable, distribution can be a problem. Lunch programs often do not aid the poorest children in that the more affluent families send their children to school, and when the truly needy *are* fed outside the home, their allotment at home is reduced. Handing out rations for women and children through health clinics often results in stretching whole families' food supplies and releasing money for other purchases, rather than supplementing the diets of the target group. Moreover, if food aid is based on donor surplus, the supply is not stable and cannot be counted on for food security.

In short, food aid is very difficult to administer equitably and needs to be guided by principles such as: (1) discernment that the aid will add to a more fair distribution of income or purchasing power among the poor (i.e. that aid will substitute for imports and so release government funds for poverty-related projects); (2) advanced planning of distribution; (3) guaranteed availability of supply; (4) selection of products that are already part of the recipients' diets; and (5) accompaniment of food aid by other monetary forms of aid (Maxwell and Singer 245).

Evaluation of Aid

When all is said and done, does it work? To the problems listed so far, more must be added. Agricultural projects are accused of bringing in technologies that can only be afforded by large farmers, thus leaving the poorest at a greater disadvantage. Bilateral (nation-nation) aid to education has stagnated since the 1970's because "there are pressures to go for 'quick return' activities rather than the long haul which education requires" (Cassen 147). Bilateral aid, in general, carries strong political obligations; tends to benefit middle-income populations through showcase, capital-intensive projects (dams, transportation systems); and often lacks provisions for recurrent costs of maintaining projects. Some countries are victims of aid overload (i.e. Haiti) where multiple projects (often duplications) have gone beyond the government's abilities to administer and coordinate activities, let alone match funds. (Donors appear and disappear in such countries, making their mark for a time, then moving on to more "interesting" projects.) Technical assistance is often beyond what recipients need and can afford to implement, and external training of selected indigenous people often leads to "brain drain." Above all else, foreign aid tends to be erratic and aims at short-term rather than long-term solutions to chronic problems.

But, on the other side, irrigation projects are highly labor-intensive in proportion to cost, and thereby generate both immediate and long-term benefits. The long-term linkages between agricultural assistance and manufacturing growth (through the increased buying power of farmers) are being studied and utilized. Aid for family planning and health education has helped substantially to reduce population growth in areas where decline in fertility is a government priority. Multilateral agencies (the U.N., World Bank) and associations of interest groups (Arab Fund for Social and Economic Development) are becoming increasingly active in the field, which reduces the kinds of politically-inspired conditions that bilateral agencies are prone to place on aid. And last, but not least, donors are learning from their mistakes. They are learning that aid policy can move toward avoidance of fragmentation through: (1) a strengthening of recipients' negotiating capacities, (2) greater coordination among donors, (3) a willingness on the part of donors to commit to long-term projects, (4) the reduction of political "leverage" on the part of donors, and (5) joint agreements between donors and recipients on long-term responsibilities for maintaining projects once they have been completed. (If roads are built, who maintains them?) (87)

Whether this movement *will* take place is dependent on many of the factors already discussed in this chapter. But it is worth ending with one further perspective outlined by Judith Tendler, after a good deal of field work in Brazil. She observes that the economic dependency of third world countries on developed countries arises from the fact that external order is imposed on a people—first through MNCs and then through the very aid agencies that claim to be liberating nations from need. She claims that the autocracy imposed by the latter is not deliberate imperialism half so much as it is a result of the corporate way of doing things. "That is, the more the donor organizations are able to impose order on the outside decision making that affects their product, the better they can perform their task" (109).

Working within and among bureaucratic, task-oriented governments, aid agencies don't know how to adjust to "the space needed by a developing country to grapple with and take charge of its destiny" (109), and so they make decisions for their clients. Ironically, then, dependency is perpetuated by a helping organization's desire to do well—on its own terms.

May we in the developed world somehow find the humility to be liberated from our obsessions as we learn from and reach out to others!

BIBLIOGRAPHY

Caporaso, James A. and Behroux Zare. "An Interpretation and Explanation of Dependency Theory," *From Dependency to Development: Strategies to Overcome Underdevelopment and Inequality,* edited by Heraldo Munoz. Boulder, Colorado: Westview Press, 1981.

Cassen, Robert and associates. *Does Aid Work?* Oxford: Clarendon Press, 1986.

Haq, Mahbub ul. *The Poverty Curtain.* New York: Columbia University Press, 1976.

———. "Beyond the Slogan of South-South Co-operation," *World Development,* 8:743–51 (1980).

———. "Negotiating a New Bargain with the Rich Countries," *From Dependency to Development.*

Jensen, Eirik G. "The Development of the Mechanized River Transport Sector in Bangladesh: Aid to the Poor," *Poverty and Aid,* edited by J.R. Parkinson. New York: St. Martins Press, 1983.

Maghoori, Raj. "Major Debates in International Relations," *Globalism vs. Realism: International Relations' Third Debate.* Boulder, Colorado: Westview Press, 1982.

Maxwell, S.J. and H.W. Singer. "Food Aid to Developing Countries: A Survey," *World Development,* 7:225–247 (1979).

Munoz, Heraldo. "Introduction: The Various Roads to Development," *From Dependency to Development.*

Rothstein, Robert L. *Global Bargaining: UNCTAD and the Quest for a New International Economic Order.* Princeton: Princeton University Press, 1979.

Streeten, Paul. "Approaches to a New International Economic Order," *World Development,* 10:1–17 (1982).

———. "Development Dichotomies," *World Development,* 11:875–889 (1983).

Stevens, Christopher. *Food Aid and the Developing World: Four African Case Studies.* New York: St. Martin's Press, 1979.

Sunkel, Osvaldo, "Developmental Styles and the Environment: An Interpretation of the Latin American Case," *From Dependency to Development.*

Waltz, Kenneth. "The Myth of National Interdependence," *Globalism vs. Realism.*

World Bank. *World Development Report, 1986.* New York: Oxford University Press, 1986.

Young, Oran. "Interdependence in World Politics," *Globalism vs. Realism.*

SUGGESTIONS FOR FURTHER STUDY

Cassen, Robert and Associates. *Does Aid Work?* Oxford: Clarendon Press, 1986.

Frankel, Francine R. *India's Green Revolution: Economic Gains and Political Costs.* Princeton: Princeton University Press, 1971.

Goulet, Denis and Michael Hudson. *The Myth of Aid.* New York: IDOC North America, 1971.

Thompson, Robert. *Green Gold: Bananas and Dependency in the Caribbean.* New York: Monthly Review Press, 1987.

DISCUSSION QUESTIONS AND ACTIVITIES

1. Start with some story-telling. Have any of you ever been involved in a friendship or other non-family relationship where you were clearly dominated by another person? What form did that domination take? Did you manage to free yourself from it without severing the relationship? How?

2. Dependency theory as it relates to nations can easily be transferred to the context of liberation movements *within* societies.

Think about the civil rights and women's movements. Separation was suggested by activists within each cause. To what extent was separation possible and/or advisable? How do you see the relationship between this and the delinking of developing countries from developed countries?

3. Ask yourselves the question: "When someone asks me for financial help, am I most likely to loan money, to give money, or to give goods in kind (clothing, food, babysitting services)?" Share your answers, with concrete examples. Then discuss what motivates each of your actions and what might be the long-term effects of each.

4. If you, as a group, had $1,000,000 to spend on foreign assistance, how would you divide the funds—geographically, functionally (in terms of target groups and activities)? Make your own chart and keep it in evidence.

5. Look over your response journals, and discuss pertinent issues raised there.

6

Domestic Aspects of Poverty

On average, per capita income in the world's developing countries rose 75 percent from 1950 to 1970. Why then has the welfare of the absolutely poor changed so little and the inequities between haves and have-nots (both within and between nations) worsened? International aspects of the problem have been discussed in the last two chapters. Domestic aspects—chiefly urbanization and militarism, with undercurrents of elitism and corruption—will be discussed here.

Urbanization

Migration/The Urban Poor

Urbanization, the change from a dispersed population pattern to concentration of populace in urban centers, may well be the primary challenge that governments of developing countries need to deal with in the next few decades. In these nations urban growth has been occurring not only on a vaster scale than in the industrialized nations, but within a much shorter time span. In 1950 sixteen percent of the population of developing countries were city dwellers; by 2000 43 percent will live in urban centers (Austin 3). These 2.12 billion persons will constitute 66 percent of city dwellers worldwide (Todaro 7). To see how this urban growth compares with that of the industrialized nations, one can study the size of Mexico City and New York from 1950 to projected figures for 2000. In 1950 Mexico City had a population of 2.9 million which was approximately one fourth of the population of New York; in 2000 Mexico City should be up to 31.6 million, an increase of approximately 29 million, which will top New York City by 9 million (Beier 66).

The most rapid urban growth will continue to take place in

cities over five million. In most of these cities in developing nations, one fourth to one half of the population already lives in "intense deprivation and denial of their basic needs" (Austin 3). Clearly the challenge to governments of third world nations is not only to absorb increased population but to insure their physical well-being and their productivity.

What are the causes of rapid urbanization in the developing world? A number of causes are cited, but rural to urban migration is the one most often discussed and analyzed. Migrants from the rural sector to the urban sector tend to be under thirty and better educated than non-migrants. They come to the cities because of an increasing shortage of land available for low-income rural population, in some cases because of civil strife in rural areas, and because of "the widespread diffusion of modern communications and transportation which encourages population movement by providing information concerning urban opportunities and reduces the cost of migration" (Beier 58). The problem is that "urban opportunities" presented in the media often turn out to be false promises for migrants who bring very few job skills with them.

At present migration counts for from one third to one half of urban growth in developing countries; by 2000 it will account for half in almost all cases. The other half will come from population growth.

A persistent question is whether governments of developing countries should encourage urbanization? In the past, urbanization has been seen as a way to bring a people out of their conservative folk traditions and into a world of industrialization and "progress." Cities, modeled after western cities, have a different spirit than the countryside; new ideas about production, consumption and social institutions are disseminated there. Education and other basic services are more readily available in urban areas. Industries are encouraged to develop in cities through protective policies, and key political decision-making groups are concentrated there as well.

Yet, despite these advantages, urban areas have become incubators for intense frustration and despair. Job shortages in the cities have been a persistent problem. Migrants come seeking work, but only the skilled succeed; others can "only get employment in activities with very low productivity or swell the ranks of the unemployed" (Sovani 326). Those who find work in industry tend to do better than they would in the rural sector due to minimum wages and union rates. But industry has not solved the employment problem for the masses of unskilled laborers.

Crowded slum neighborhoods in urban centers are particularly prone to health threats, and contaminated water supplies spread disease quickly. In addition, nutrition tends to fall off among city dwellers. In cities, food must be purchased, and many other items compete for what little money exists in households. Traditional foods are less available, while more expensive, processed foods are offered and appealingly advertised. There is a decline in breastfeeding in urban centers due to mothers' work and to the higher status connected with bottle feeding (Austin 38). Families have irregular schedules and need to conserve on fuel, which disrupt regular preparation of meals.

Transportation systems are rarely able to keep up with urban growth. Yet as cities get larger, and as people are increasingly settled in outlying areas, the need for inexpensive transportation to the center where most employment is still offered is essential.

Housing, however, is the biggest urban problem that governments of developing countries must face. In large older cities, accessible land is scarce and expensive. It is cheaper on the outskirts, but services are weak in these areas and, as already stated, transportation to the center is a problem. In addition, the unemployed often do not have money to buy land. Therefore, a good deal of urban settlement occurs "spontaneously" in unplanned squatter camps and shantytowns that provide no public services. Nearly one half of the population of Mexico City and of Ankara live in such neighborhoods, and they are not radical exceptions (Turner 507). Programs of slum clearance, while they offer aesthetic and social advantages, often legislate against the poor because they need to be relocated (where?) during bulldozing and rebuilding and then may not be able to afford the rents in new structures. Planned, legal squatter settlements and slum upgrading are more practical solutions, while not improving the appearance of third world cities.

Recognizing all of the problems that accompany rapid urban growth, some development theorists argue that governments of poor countries encourage migration from the rural to the urban sector erroneously, against their own gain. These theorists blame this discrepancy on a phenomenon they call "urban bias."

Urban Bias/The Rural Poor

Urban bias is a prejudicial preference for what takes place in cities. As Michael Todaro argues, while rural to urban migration is an inevitable and at times a desirable part of development, "the tendency of most developing world governments to focus their development efforts on one or two main cities—often to the neglect of their rural areas—has created distortions and imbalances in both economic and social opportunities in urban and rural areas" (17). Michael Lipton claims that urban bias often results from a willingness on the part of developing countries to pursue economic growth at the expense of human welfare and the alleviation of poverty. It also results from an inclination to pursue economic growth on the terms that brought it about in the developed world—industrialization: "They want to modernize fast: they rightly assume that rich nations are non-agricultural and that their own agriculture is poor; and they wrongly conclude that rapid industrialization at the expense of agriculture can produce rapid development" (63).

But what we are talking about here is not industrial bias; it is *urban* bias. More is at stake than factories. Decision making in poor countries tends to come from "small groups of articulate, organized or powerful people in regular contact with senior officials and politicians" (61). These groups (labor leaders, money managers, academics, editors, radio producers, transportation engineers, service workers, journalists) live in the cities. They may support the industrial enterprise but are not working in industrial occupations.

Having the power groups so centralized in urban areas gives a degree of political stability to poor countries. Labor becomes a kind of "aristocracy" of the poor—the urban *un*employed are politically disenfranchised while the rural poor are spread out, hard to hear, and easy to control. Yet stability may be purchased at the price of damaging inequalities. As Michael Lipton claims, then, the major conflict in these countries is not between labor and management but between the rural poor and urban employer and proletariat (as a cooperative group).

Resources are destructively diverted from the rural to the urban sector in a number of ways. The chief one is pricing: "It is above all by cheapening farm outputs that both private and public powers transfer savings capacity from agriculture to the rest of the economy" (293). Urban employers lobby for low food prices because they want their work forces to be strong and well-fed on little money. Urban workers want low food prices so that they can spend wages on other items. But the rural sector is demoralized and impoverished through cheap food. Food prices are often kept low while non-farm prices are kept high, so that farm families make less income but need more cash for non-food subsistence items. Cheap food transfers rural surplus to the urban centers.

Resources are directed to these centers from the rural periphery in other ways. Since there is less personal saving in the rural sector (money is spent on family needs and on farm supplies), some administrators in developing countries advocate taxing farmers. As they argue, this would cut back on private spending and forcibly increase *public* saving and investment. What is often ignored in this analysis is that farmers are more likely to engage in private investment in their own means of production than urban dwellers, so that instead of encouraging overall investment, taxation of farmers limits investment to the public sector, which usually means city projects. In addition, taxes are rarely adjusted to account for fluctuations in household income, which in the farming sector can be considerable from year to year; thus farmers become victims of an inflexible economic system.

Also, urban areas get progressive, skills-oriented education and are the centers of higher education. (In developing countries institutions of higher education rarely engage in agricultural research.) This encourages selective migration from rural to urban areas. As Lipton points out, the problem with urbanization of the population in developing countries is often not *how many* go, but *who* goes—educated young people and those who can afford the move. The "successes stay while the rest return" which, of course, depletes not only material resources in the rural sector, but human resources as well. With the depletion of human resources comes increased passivity which is exacerbated by geographic isolation and debilitating patterns of economic discrimination. Thus the rural sector tends to be apolitical, a factor which poets over the years have erroneously praised as enviable innocence.

Yet romantic poets are not the only persons who do not see the rural sector with clear vision. For many government administrators, journalists and representatives from aid agencies, "there are major obstacles to perceiving the nature and extent of rural poverty in Third World centers. These obstacles originate not only in the nature of rural poverty itself, but also in the condition of these, not themselves of the rural poor, who do or more significantly, do not perceive that poverty" (Chambers 2). That is, those with the power to do something about the inequities between the urban-industrial core and the rural-agricultural periphery are themselves products of the center. They are people used to and biased by the workings of power, prestige, professionalism and academic analysis. When they visit rural areas, they see what they want to see and what lower level civil servants have prepared for them to see. They take with them a spatial bias, rarely traveling off the main roads into the heart of poverty; a project bias; a bias for progressive farmers—those who use services and adopt new projects; a male bias; a bias for polite and articulate "informants"; and a dry season bias. "The plight of a poor widow starving and sick in the wet season in remote and inaccessible area may never in any way impinge on the consciousness of anyone outside her own community" (10).

The very things that make rural poverty what it is—lack of assets, physical weakness of the population, vulnerability to economic contingencies, political powerlessness, and geographic isolation—make it too cumbersome to fit any given diagnostic paradigm. In addition, government administrators and civil servants who want to be on "the cutting edge" of economic growth do not want to invest time and money in what seems to be a vestige of the past.

The question remains, then: What can be done about the urban squalor that has resulted from rural to urban migration, and what can simultaneously make substantial development of the agricultural sector more attractive (or in some cases, even an evident necessity) to third world countries and thus stem the tide of unnecessary migration?

Domestic Solutions to Urban and Rural Poverty

Given the rapid growth of cities, governments of developing countries need to give more thought to urban planning. Policies need to be established for migration control, infrastructure development, the location and control of industry, and decentralization of civic decision-making. Practical projects for legitimization of land tenure, slum upgrading, "sites and services" planning, generation of employment, and the deployment of basic services need to be enacted.

Decent housing and a healthy environment for poor city dwellers ought to be a major priority; this kind of development can create jobs for the very persons it serves. "Sites and services" projects prepare settlements for squatters. Small plots of urban land are leveled, furnished with roads, services, schools and clinics. Families can build on those plots, rent free as in Madras, or with a small land rent as in Calcutta. Ideally, small-scale industries should be encouraged in these areas through low-interest loans.

Where unplanned, unhealthy squatter settlements already exist, they can be upgraded—provided with utilities, with sanitary latrines, and with clinics and schools. While slum-upgrading is not a long-term solution, it is a recognition that public housing is too expensive for the poorest, it increases the immediate welfare of these people substantially, and it represents a "cost-effective use of scarce resources" (Richardson 136).

Governments need to consider strategies for decentralizing cities, for making jobs and markets available in a variety of reachable areas, thus releasing pressure on transportation systems. Ironically, this phase of urban planning may be more difficult for democratic regimes than for more autocratic ones, for the process will involve policies unpopular to various lobby groups and will require long-term implementation surveillance, which short-term, elected regimes may not be able to provide (143).

Then there is the task of reversing the flow of resources from the urban to the rural sector. Concentration on urban problems alone will perpetuate the allure of the city, inspire further migration, increase urban problems and further impoverish rural families. Meanwhile, investment in rural life can efficiently alleviate poverty, promote human dignity, and help to balance population.

Poverty is more evenly spread over rural areas than it is in urban centers where "[the] unemployed, beggars, prostitutes, and unorganized service workers employed in such activities such as shoe-cleaning, laundry and domestic service" tend to congregate in destitute pockets (Lipton 54). This means that poverty-oriented projects in the *rural* sector can serve an entire demographic area and thus lead efficiently to community growth. In addition, the rural poor are usually at least seasonally employed, while a large number of the urban poor are unemployed. Government funds to increase productivity work best in areas where people have jobs. Because farmers live so close to what they do, aid to farming communities stands to alleviate need and increase productivity simultaneously. Furthermore, aid to farmers holds out the promise of being self-generating, in that recipients tend to invest extra income in productive ways (seeds, fertilizer, irrigation systems, equipment).

How can this turnabout happen? Maintenance of incentive food prices is an obvious first step. Careful administration of food aid so that surplus does not reduce equitable food prices, and so that income from sale of food goes into the agricultural sector is another possibility. Liberalization of loans to farmers is a further action governments can take. To be progressive, these loans should avoid insistence on "productive" use. (General maintenance of family and equipment may be a primary need.) Lenders should accept a wide range of securities, provide for extension, have realistic interest rates, and demand repayment (Lipton 300). In addition to loans, governments can encourage urban private investment in rural projects through Rural Finance Corporations.

In terms of "ownership of policy," rural communities should be encouraged to organize and become articulate about their needs. Peasant movements are more effective when they concentrate on urban-rural problems rather than peasant-peasant conflict. Farm labor movements and coalitions of small rural businesses could set themselves the task of lobbying for economic change.

For any of this to take place, of course, administrative attitudes and actions will have to change. Civil service agencies could assign the best entrants to rural posts as a general rule, give extra pay for rural postings, provide for longer postings to rural areas, and make more effort to reward outstanding performances in outlying areas. Governments could put more money into rural planning and provide money for agricultural research. They could be more public about rural success and information.

In addition, rural information gathering could be more intentional and widely-based. "Visiting" officials could work harder at overcoming social and spatial biases, stay longer and act less important (thus obtaining more accurate information and less "official" responses). Civil servants could do more in-service research as part of their training, thus "learning from" while "working with." Even simulation games employing rural problems could become part of general administrative consciousness raising.

All of these individual actions and reforms could lead to important long-term policy changes: (1) a nutritional emphasis on agricultural output (crops with high caloric yield rather than those that cater to tastes of urbanites); (2) a general reduction of anti-rural pricing schemes; rural access to education; (3) equitable availability of health care, electricity, water; (4) government publication of rates of return on agricultural production (which might well encourage private urban investment); (5) clearly defined targets for public investment; (6) allocation of public monies for rural and agricultural research; and (7) public emphasis on mini-farms (Lipton 342).

The last policy change listed takes us directly to the issue of land reform and its goals. Land reform is generally employed by a government regime to distribute and manage lands more equitably. A land reform program may have to address the feudalistic landlord and tenant system of Asia, the Latin American system of large farms, and communal landownership patterns of tribal groups in Africa. Reform might mean changes in the rights of tenants, changes in landlords, subdivision of large landholdings, and transfer of land to the state or from the state to individuals. It is particularly useful in areas where land is being underutilized under the "old system" (*The Assault on World Poverty* 193).

Research on size of holdings indicates that "Productivity and land—defined as yield per hectare—is generally higher on smaller holdings than on larger holdings" (*The Assault on World Poverty* 196). A caution, however, is that smallholder farmers consume more of their own produce than large farmers and so leave less for the market. Therefore, in redistribution of land, the size of plots should be calculated to provide for the physiological need of a farm family and a surplus for sale to urban consumers.

A final consideration is what developed countries can do to facilitate domestic readjustments of the inequities between urban and rural sectors. They can provide direct, long-term aid for agriculture, de-emphasize the exportation of labor-replacing farm technology, and liberalize restrictions on agricultural exports (i.e. textiles and processed foods) even where competition is involved. But as Lipton concludes, their roles must be contextual rather than interventionist: "Our duty is to attempt to make the policies of our own countries more helpful to poor people in poor countries" (352).

Militarism

The prominent use of military force to secure and promote political power in third world countries is a recognized phenomenon that inspires several reactions. Radicals argue that organized force in third world countries has been created and is maintained to facilitate the integration of developing countries into the capitalist system. In this view, third world militaries are perceived as a major *cause* of underdevelopment. They protect multinational corporations, maintain political stability at any cost, absorb large amounts of domestic assets, and are overly dependent on first world models. More moderate views acknowledge these points, but qualify them through consideration of the internal dynamics of third world countries.

In all, the factor that appears to distinguish the military in developing countries from armies in developed centers is their involvement in economic and political systems. Leaving room for many individual differences, the military establishment in third world nations tends to be closely integrated into economic and political policy. They accomplish this not only through standing armies but through paramilitary and police forces as well. First we will look at overt military involvement in government, then at paramilitary forces.

The Role of the Armed Forces

Colonial rule was more bureaucratic than military. So colonial territories not only had ineffective indigenous military forces, but their military institutions were not infused with strong codes of conduct and concepts of military professionalism. This means that with independence, governments and military structures were often forced to develop simultaneously which established a kind of symbiosis between them not common in the developed world: "The more or less simultaneous development of the armed forces and the ruling party in the course of an independence or liberation struggle also encourages co-operation between the military and civilian sectors of the government" (Ball 570). The need for political stability and national security in new nations encouraged the military's continual involvement in domestic development. But since "no military-dominated government, not even one as entrenched as that of Thailand, Indonesia or Brazil, can administer a country solely with military manpower," the collaboration of the civil service with the military was also necessary in even the most oligarchical states (571).

Furthermore, the connection between the military and fledgling industry was cemented early on. The military gave safety to domestic businesses which in turn supplied the growing state with capital. Military leaders interested in advancement formed "protectorates" with foreign businesses and thereby often managed to gain control of the distribution of foreign economic aid.

Various indigenous elite groups deliberately allied themselves with the military, seeking strength for their positions and aiming to squeeze out both other elites and the mass of the population. As Nicole Ball explains, "One reason for this exclusion is that elites fear that increased participation by the poor would lead to alternatives in existing political and economic situations which would be inimical to elite interests." Capitalism is the friend of both military and economic elites in these countries because it allows "a relatively small group of individuals to control the political and economic systems of a country" (572).

Through overlapping alliances, with the ruling party, civil service, domestic and foreign business, and indigenous elites, the military in developing countries assures its own future. Because it has a "monopoly over the means of violence," the military can command a large amount of the nation's material resources— supplying salaries, new equipment and facilities—for a rising number of personnel. Understandably, military coups in third world countries (a common phenomenon) usually result in a dramatic rise in military expenditures. (For example, the coup against Nkrumah's government in Ghana, 1966–69, brought about a 22 percent rise in military expenditures, and one wonders to what extent Nkrumah's austerity budget for defense spending occasioned the takeover in the first place. [573]) This, of course, causes a siphoning off of government revenues to the military establishment and the growth of discontent. Nevertheless, officers claim the necessity of military takeovers because "civilians have proven inefficient, corrupt and generally incapable of governing and the country is, as a result, plagued by widespread social, economic and political disorder" (574). A military coup is almost always a move away from political liberalization because liberalization would bring with it reduction of military expenditures in order to promote education, health care, and other welfare projects. It would also bring a cutback on subsidies to industries run by the military and a purge of military personnel.

Liberalization is particularly frightening to persons seeking personal power and wealth through military rank. In most third world countries the military is still a means by which the sons of the poor and middle classes can find personal advancement. But since this advancement often comes at the price of bribery, rake-offs, and other forms of corruption, loss of military power in a nation could bring imprisonment as well as "unemployment."

For their part, the governments of industrialized countries often welcome military rule in developing countries because it provides "stable governments"—governments that can protect multinational corporations, private lending corporations, and foreign military bases. Such governments can also be "depended on" for continuous supplies of raw materials. Therefore, in the Soviet Union, military aid to developing countries since World War II has equaled economic aid, and in the United States it has run two to three times the economic aid budget.

In short, it is doubtful that the persuasive influence of the military is going to decline in the near future in developing countries, which means that projects to alleviate poverty are going to have to compete with a variety of internally and externally supported, stability-oriented structures.

The Role of Paramilitary Agencies

Military structures in developing countries are complex organizations made up of armies and a variety of paramilitary forces. This accounts for a good deal of their strength; ". . . the national military forces were able to seize and exercise power because they could assume that they had the tacit support of the existing police and paramilitary forces. The latter, in turn, were able to exercise sufficient control to permit the military to restructure regions without explosive violence" (Janowitz 16). Paramilitary units often include national police forces, local defense units and workers' militias. Their task is generally to control politically disruptive groups or resistance to the central regime. They watch minorities for signs of unrest and form fairly strong bargaining units of their own. Morris Janowitz gives them particular credit for the "military's role as agents of social and political change" (107).

What results is a number of developing countries with either a military oligarchy or a civilian government with a strong coercive/military element. In either case, one does not have totalitarianism in its fully developed sense (Nazi Germany, Stalinist Russia). Totalitarianism is more "pervasive and sophisticated"—often calling for imprisonment of large numbers of civilians in concentration camps. The coercive system of developing nations is more a function of an "elite perspective on the pace and direction of internal sociopolitical change" (33) than of ideology. "Undesirables" are expelled, threatened, or impoverished which makes concentration camps unnecessary. That is, the values of a powerful, usually wealthy minority are institutionalized in a persuasive, interlocked system of repressive control. National life is controlled in a variety of ways, making the country appear stable and mixing civilian and military interests in a nexus of protective policies. Unfortunately, this protection rarely extends to the most vulnerable.

Elitism and Corruption

Elitism hardly has to be discussed as a separate phenomenon in developing countries. It has been discussed as an offshoot of colonial bureaucracy, as a factor in the inequities of economic growth, as a reason behind urban bias, and as both a civilian and a military political force. Basically, an elite is a group of people who have prestige through education, money, and/or political power and who seek advantages because of that prestige. The elites in developing countries tend to ally themselves with comparable elements in the rich nations and to further core/periphery divisions within nations as well as between nations.

Leftist analysts, with a good deal of logic behind them, connect elitism with the capitalist bias of the western nations, a system that often seems to be based upon the survival of the fittest and, in many social contexts, can center power, land, and money in the hands of a few. But to be fair, one also has to look at pre-colonial patterns, often involving autocratic tribal hierarchies or religious caste systems, not to speak of the common manifestations of aggression throughout human history. True, through media promotion of consumer values, first world nations export a style of life that only a few can achieve and promote desires for the urban "good life," but indigenous cultural practices often promote elitism as well.

As with the rich nation/poor nation syndrome, sacrifice of self-interest as well as forced investment in poverty-oriented programs can help to combat elitism. The development of the negotiating powers of previously powerless groups is also an important element. Efficiency and equity *can* be two sides of the same coin, but not without great internal effort and external support for a new interdependency of social classes.

This brings us to one last consideration, one connected with all elitism, militarism, and political power—corruption. Corruption exists in all countries, developing and developed alike, but when businesses are growing without formulated policy checks, when rival elites control various land and money sectors, when military and paramilitary alliances control whole populations, corruption is bound to be a factor in economic imbalances, and corruption is often a factor contributing to discontent and military coups.

The masses may initially welcome a military-dominated government which promises an end to corruption and progress for the poor, but the corrupt practices are usually reinstated and new coalitions of civilian and military elites stage counter-coups. Part of this recurring problem is that the involvement of the military in the political system provides "opportunities" for military personnel to advance themselves personally. These opportunities are greatest when the military controls the political process, but civilian leaders may also, when in power, ingratiate themselves to military leaders by offering them such opportunities. Thus corruption, elitism, first world business interests, and military involvement in government feed (and feed on) one another in political systems that are still finding their way in a world that holds out unrealizable consumer goals for anyone who can afford a radio or a popular magazine. Meanwhile, the poor in rural areas live hidden desperate lives that, once acknowledged, pose serious moral and economic problems to regimes that have suffered coup after coup in a search for stability. (From 1961–66, 71 successful coups occurred in Africa and 44 in Latin America; from 1966–76, 51 occurred in Africa and 23 in Latin America [Frank 293].)

Perhaps the clue to genuine domestic stability is the same as that offered at the end of Chapter Five—a lucid assessment of indigenous problems and factions, recognition of a need for control that may be legitimate years away from democracy, disavowal of "impossible" lifestyles, and taxation of the rich rather than the poor. Then (even simultaneously) in a non-imitative fashion, and having attempted to clean up whatever colonial residue is left, developing countries may be in a position to negotiate an end to immoral, inefficient disparities between nations.

BIBLIOGRAPHY

The Assault on World Poverty, The World Bank Group. Baltimore: Johns Hopkins University Press, 1975.

Austin, James E. *Confronting Urban Malnutrition: The Design of Nutrition Programs,* World Bank Staff Occasional Papers, no. 8. Baltimore: Johns Hopkins University Press, 1980.

Ball, Nicole. "The Military in Politics: Who Benefits and How," *World Development,* 9:569–582 (1981).

Beier, George J. "Can Third World Cities Cope?" *Urban Development in the Third World,* edited by Pradip K. Ghosh. Westport, Connecticut: Greenwood Press, 1984.

Chambers, Robert. "Rural Poverty Unperceived: Problems and Remedies," *World Development,* 9:1–19 (1981).

Frank, Andre Gunder. *Crisis in the Third World.* New York: Holmes and Meier Publications, 1981.

Grimes, Orville F. "The Urban Housing Situation in Developing Countries," *Urban Development in the Third World.*

Hoselitz, Bert F. "The Role of Cities in the Economic Growth of Underdeveloped Countries," *The City in Newly Developing Countries: Readings on Urbanism and Urbanization,* edited by Gerald Breese. Englewood Cliffs: Prentice-Hall, 1969.

Janowitz, Morris. *Military Institutions and Coercion in the Developing Nations.* Chicago: University of Chicago Press, 1977.

Lee, James A. *The Environment, Public Health, and Human Ecology: Considerations for Economic Development.* Baltimore: Johns Hopkins University Press, 1985.

Lipton, Michael. *Why Poor People Stay Poor: Urban Bias in World Development.* Cambridge: Harvard University Press, 1976.

Richardson, Harry W. "National Urban Development Strategies in Developing Countries," *Urban Development in the Third World.*

Sen, Amartya. *Poverty and Famines: An Essay on Entitlement and Deprivation.* Oxford: Clarendon Press, 1981.

Sovani, P.V. "The Analysis of Over-Urbanization," *The City in Newly Developing Countries.*

Todaro, Michael P. "Urbanization in Developing Nations," *Urban Development in the Third World.*

Turner, John F.C. "Uncontrolled Urban Settlement: Problems and Policies," *The City in Newly Developing Countries.*

SUGGESTIONS FOR FURTHER STUDY

Aziz, Sartaj. *Rural Development: Learning from China.* New York: Holmes and Meier Publications, 1978.

Breese, Gerald. *Urbanization in Newly Developing Countries.* Englewood Cliffs: Prentice-Hall, 1966.

Janowitz, Morris. *Military Institutions and Coercion in the Developing Nations.* Chicago: University of Chicago Press, 1977.

Lieuwen, Edwin. *Generals vs. Presidents: Neo-militarism in Latin America.* New York: Praeger, 1974.

Lipton, Michael. *Why Poor People Stay Poor: Urban Bias in World Development.* Cambridge: Harvard University Press, 1976.

DISCUSSION QUESTIONS AND ACTIVITIES

1. Consider getting together with Monopoly sets and playing for an evening. When you are finished, discuss the feelings that accompanied "getting rich" and "going out." Those who won can articulate for the rest the "elite mentality" and those who lost the "poverty mentality." Remind yourselves that while, for you, gross disparities are part of a game, for others it is reality.

2. What has your experience been with the "homeless" of our cities? Have you been merely a spectator? Or have you tried to speak with and understand the backgrounds of these people? Share your experiences and discuss how housing and services for the destitute can become part of city planning.

3. What are your "off the cuff" experiences of rural life? Are they more idyllic or dreary? Where did they come from? What distinguishes, in your experience, pleasing rural life from "back-

ward" existence. Try to apply some of these observations to the situation of rural life in third world countries.

4. Share stories about your various experiences with the military—from a parent's role in World War II to a visit to a military state with frequent check points. Would a close alliance between military and political power make you feel more secure or less secure? Why?

5. Bring in someone from Habitat for Humanity or another cooperative assistance service group—one that has projects in poor rural areas. Have the person speak to you about the "hidden" rural poor in your own country and others that he or she knows about.

6. Read quickly over your response journals and discuss relevant issues that appear there.

PART III

A REALISTIC LOOK
AT STRATEGIES FOR SUSTAINED RESPONSE

7

International Organizations

Since the very beginning of this study, we have been wrestling with the tension between the centripetal demands of self, tribe, and nation-state, and the centrifugal demands of others, universal values, and globalism. The title and preface state quite clearly that self-development and global concerns are intimately connected. Chapter Two argues that unless universalism balances tribalism in a given value system, that system will be lopsided and deficient in its assessment of human dignity. Meanwhile Chapters Four, Five, and Six caution against pseudo or coercive internationalism which promotes economic and political collectivism at the expense of poor nations and indigenous cultural values.

One area where the argument for universalism is essential is that of international law. When the concepts of national sovereignty and "self-determination" of individual states become so ensconced in our thinking that they are used to defend large-scale violations of human rights by specific regimes and domestic policies that clearly legislate against the poor, they have become false doctrine. Hitler's regime did not have the right to shape a society on the basis of racial selection. The government of Ethiopia does not have the right to distribute food aid on the basis of the political alliances of the starving. The United Nations ought to denounce such domestic policies in the name of human dignity.

Likewise, persons seeking solutions to global poverty ought to reflect on the nature of international organizations, for no individual or group of individuals in the first world has the power to effect change without moving across national lines, intellectually and functionally. Perhaps one of the best arguments for such a move comes from Henri Dunant, founder of the Red Cross, who back in the middle of the nineteenth century argued that those wounded in war are no longer partisan; they have, by their very neediness, been rendered neutral and, along with their physicians and nurses, ought to be given transnational status.

Of course, no one born in a particular place and raised with a particular set of values can ever be considered truly non-partisan, but the absolutely needy and the persons who wish to respond to that need must participate in a process of growth that does not place narrow national interests first. The determination and protection of human rights is not an issue that can be left solely to the arbitrary will of each state. What we will be discussing in this chapter is a variety of international organizations that claim to be doing something significant for international development. It will be up to you to assess their claims and to decide which you will support.

There are several important categories of international organizations. Intergovernment organizations (IGOs) are organizations formed by members of governments from two or more sovereign states with the purpose of pursuing a common interest. The United Nations is possibly the best example of such an organization. International non-governmental organizations (INGOs) are organizations formed by non-governmental representatives of groups with a common purpose from more than two countries. The International Red Cross is a good example of this type. Private voluntary organizations (PVOs), usually called non-governmental organizations (NGOs) outside of the United States, are organizations formed by like-minded individuals whose interests are international. Oxfam America is a clear example of a PVO. That leaves multinational corporations (MNCs). Do they belong in such a study? Their primary purpose is not international community, nor would that be appropriate. Yet they exert more power over the international community than most of the groups mentioned above, and they claim to have a direct positive role in international economic growth. For these reasons, they have been included.

In addition to there being several *types* of international organizations, they can *function* in a number of ways. They can function as instruments for individual members to seek their own ends. International organizations also function as arenas for dialogue between members, "places for members to come together to discuss, argue, cooperate, or disagree" (Archer 11). Finally, international organizations can be actors, that is, they can take unified action that arises out of the purposes of the group itself.

The following discussion of international organizations is in no way exhaustive. The fact is that there are at least 300 intergovernmental organizations and over 3,000 international nongovernmental organizations in existence. We propose to look at some of the most influential in the field of economic and social development, and we hope that further study takes readers into a more expansive understanding of how such networks can and ought to work.

Intergovernmental Organizations (IGOs)

The United Nations

It is difficult to discuss the United Nations without first looking at the League of Nations. The League of Nations grew out of concerns generated by World War I, primarily peace-keeping concerns. Woodrow Wilson's fourteenth point in his famous Fourteen Points stated: "A general association of nations must be formed under specific covenants for the purpose of affording mutual guarantees of political independence and territorial integrity to great and small States alike" (Bennett 17). These points were generally well received by the European community, and the League covenant became part of the Treaty of Versailles. While the main goals of the League were to promote peace and prevent war, some recognition was given to the necessity of economic and social cooperation between nations. Ironically, the United States was the only major power that never joined.

World War II destroyed the functional effectiveness of the League, but out of its ashes rose the United Nations, "primarily a peace and security organization based on the concept of Four Policemen, that is, the USA, USSR, the United Kingdom and China as protectors of the world against a recurrence of Axis aggression" (Archer 24). Since 1945, the number of states and state-types seeking membership has increased substantially. From 51 members in 1945, the U.N. went to 100 in 1969 and over 160 at present. Member nations tend to divide into east-west/north-south blocs, but the north includes the USSR which claims to have a unique relationship with nations of the south because of its non-participation in colonialism. Moreover, OPEC nations are part of the south's "Group of 77" (the nations who originally called for a New International Economic Order), but they have obtained a good deal of wealth at the expense of third world nations.

The three main goals of the U.N. are: (1) to maintain international peace and security, (2) to provide for economic and social cooperation among nations, and (3) to promote respect for human rights for all people. In order to achieve these goals, the organization is divided into five primary bodies and a whole series of subsidiary organizations. The chart illustrates how these various parts interrelate. We will discuss, in brief, the functions of the five major bodies, concentrating most of our attention on the Economic and Social Council.

The six primary bodies of the U.N. are: the General Assembly, the Security Council, the Secretariat, the Economic and Social Council, the Trusteeship Council, and the International Court of Justice. The General Assembly is the most active body of the organization. Here all members gather to discuss issues and recommend actions, to decide financial matters, to elect members of other branches, and to process recommendations for general membership. The Security Council, made up of the U.S., USSR, United Kingdom, China, and France, plus ten non-permanent members, oversees international peace and security and recommends nations for membership. The Secretariat is a body of civil servants that "takes care of business." The International Court of Justice hears cases submitted by individual states and gives legal advice to other branches of the U.N. The Trusteeship Council, practically defunct in our time, supervises non-self-governing territories. That leaves the Economic and Social Council (ECOSOC) which is the branch of U.N. work most valuable for this study.

The mission of ECOSOC is "to promote the welfare of all people everywhere": to research causes and solutions of economic and social problems, to recommend action, and to coordinate the activities of its subsidiary organizations. These subsidiaries cover human rights, refugees, economic and social development, culture, education, health, food supply, trade and transportation,

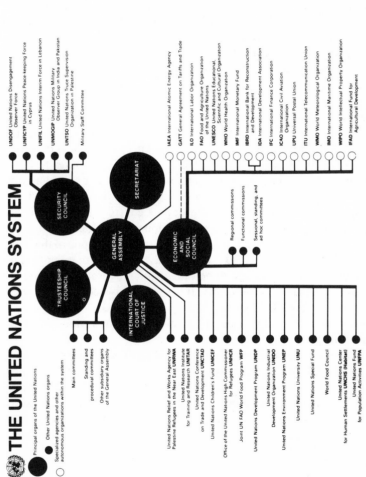

Worldmark Encyclopedia of the Nations, 6th ed. Vol. I: *United Nations*. NY: John Wiley & Sons, 1984.

population, drugs, housing, communications, and labor. It is no surprise that ECOSOC controls four fifths of the U.N. budget and has more subsidiaries than any other major body. Such emphasis illustrates that during its short lifetime, the U.N. has moved markedly from a policy of post-World War II "recovery" to one of "development," in response to the fact that since 1945, the gap between the industrialized and developing nations has widened substantially and that it continues to grow broader every year.

Of the 160 some nations that belong to the U.N., two thirds are underdeveloped. In order to serve them, ECOSOC seeks to educate and influence the attitudes of its more affluent members (the U.N. has become the world's largest publisher of development materials); it sponsors demonstration and pilot projects; it seeks development funding from external aid sources; and it promotes trade at stable and remunerative prices. One of its more active subsidiaries is the United Nations International Children's Fund (UNICEF). Started in 1947 with $15 million dollars contributed by the U.S., UNICEF now handles funds from members, non-member nations and private individuals. Because of its clear focus on one of the most vulnerable groups of persons and because of its international membership, UNICEF may well be one of the most successful philanthropic organizations in history. It has even spawned its own source of funding; in 1988 alone the U.S. Committee for UNICEF raised over $4.8 million in the sale of greeting cards for various development projects.

UNICEF notwithstanding, ECOSOC's budget does not allow it to provide the loans or grants needed for many of the major development programs it recommends. As indicated earlier, it primarily provides pre-investment needs—information, demonstration projects, advice, and training. For major funding of projects it depends on two other major IGOs: the World Bank and the International Monetary Fund.

World Bank

The International Bank for Reconstruction and Development, or World Bank, was founded on June 25, 1946 to assist in the reconstruction of Europe and Japan and in the development of the "less developed" world. In the early years of the Bank, the tendency was to equate development with economic growth, and so the Bank invested primarily in transportation systems, communication, development of ports, and power projects. From 1961 to 1965, 76.8 percent of their lending was for electrical power or transportation, while only 6 percent went for agricultural development. When Robert McNamara took over as President in the late 1960's, development lending grew fivefold, and the staff almost doubled. Under his tutelege, the Bank became increasingly devoted to the alleviation of poverty, as over against economic growth. It began to invest in subsistence agriculture, in rural development, basic education, health, low-cost housing—all of the things described in Chapter Three as long term development needs. By 1981, 31 percent of the total lending of the Bank was for agricultural and rural development, most with a "small-farmer element or component" (Ayers 5). In addition, the Bank added more staff from developing countries and developed its research units substantially.

What caused such a change? Economic growth, where it had occurred in the developing world, had often by-passed the poor and sometimes increased their plight. Unemployment and underemployment had increased, while agriculture, particularly subsistence agriculture, had been ignored. The major goal of the Bank remained modernization through capitalist approaches to development, but alleviation of poverty had become a major focus.

Is such a combination of goals possible? Critics of the left and the right say no, for different reasons. Leftist critics of the Bank claim that the real solution to poverty lies "in the revolutionary uprooting of the dependent capitalist system and its wholesale replacement by some variant of socialism" (Ayers 11). Conservative critics claim that the Bank undermines capitalist development by supporting state planning efforts and failing to push a market-orientation to development. In light of all of this, it seems fair to characterize the efforts of the World Bank as neither revolutionary nor reactionary, but reformist, within a capitalist framework.

How does the Bank work? There are three members in the World Bank group: the World Bank itself, the International Finance Corporation (IFC), and the International Development Association (IDA). The IFC promotes the growth of private enterprises in developing countries. The IDA is the "soft-loan affiliate" of the Bank, granting long-term, interest-free credits to the poorest countries. (While a regular Bank loan comes with an interest rate of 11.6 percent and runs for fifteen to twenty years, an IDA grant bears only a service charge of 0.75 percent and runs for fifty years.)

The World Bank proper has three basic functions. First, it functions as a marketplace of ideas about poverty and development. Annual addresses of the president, policy papers prepared by various research departments, and annual *World Development Reports* provide helpful information about the current status of global welfare. As a second function, the World Bank furnishes member nations with country-specific development information and economic analyses. Third, the Bank loans money for the implementation of development projects.

Compared with the total amount of money needed for third world development, the World Bank's investments are small, yet its international status and research component give it tremendous weight as a proponent of alternative development strategies and as a catalyst for self-development. Whether the Bank carries out these roles with success and integrity is a topic that its critics on the left and the right will surely be debating for some time.

It is equally clear that political differences will continue to constrain a good deal of the Bank's activities. The Bank is constantly faced with investing in regimes whose policies are not conducive to the development of democracy nor to the type of economic development that the Bank envisions. This raises several questions. If a country's official policies virtually ignore the plight of the poor, will loans for projects aimed at alleviation of poverty do that much good? Moreover, what happens to the maintenance of these projects once the Bank's role is completed? If the poor themselves welcome these projects, will the poor be able to lobby successfully for their extension and thereby help to change regime policy?

Then, of course, there are the political differences between subscribing member nations. Since a nation's voting power rests with the magnitude of its Bank subscription (comparable to shares of stock in a corporation), wealthy nations control Bank policy. This factor encourages Bank personnel to measure success by the amount of money moved (the number of loans made and retrieved) rather than by the success of projects to alleviate poverty.

Finally, there are substantial ideological differences among members of the Bank staff. For example, even with the commitment to invest in the alleviation of poverty during the McNamara years, there were distinct differences between staff members who favored the more conservative approach of "redistribution with growth" (RWG) and those who favored the "basic needs approach" (BNA). The RWG strategy stressed a necessary link between international and intranational equity. That is, one needed to concentrate on an increase in national wealth (GNP), along with a closing of the gap between the rich and poor within nations. The BNA called for a clear focus on providing for the needs of the poor. This approach often entailed more government intervention in the marketplace, since markets that catered to the wants of the privileged would have to be expanded to markets that provided sufficient basic goods for the populace at large. Many staff members felt that the basic needs approach was a masked call for revolution and could not be implemented by a reformist, non-interventionist organization. Thus, the RWG strategy was adopted. Robert Ayers' assessment of this choice is probably an accurate one: "The adoption of redistribution with growth only partly changed the nature of the institution. The adoption of the main alternative approach to poverty alleviation would have completely transformed it" (91). There were, of course, some folks who thought that transformation was exactly what the World Bank needed, but the subscribing nations backed restricted change.

Practically speaking, what kind of anti-poverty work does the Bank promote in rural areas? Loans with small collateral demands are made available to small farmers. Farmers are educated in agricultural extension programs that encourage them to increase production through the use of fertilizers, irrigation, and new varieties of seeds. New roads make transport of products easier. Primary education and health services increase the quality of life.

Yet there are many problems associated with rural projects. Lending to small farmers carries little benefit for landless peasants.

Moreover, to be really successful, programs of support for the rural sector need to be preceded by effective land reform measures. If the recipient nation has no interest in agrarian reform, the Bank is helpless to aid the *most* needy.

Practically, what kind of anti-poverty work does the Bank promote in urban areas? It invests in small-scale enterprise enhancement programs, utilities, transportation, education, health services, housing development, slum upgrading, and water/sanitation projects.

A major drawback to many of these activities is that they do not generate hard cash with which the borrowing nation can pay back the loan. Thus governments without clear poverty programs prefer to borrow for more profitable ventures than building water systems for customers whose water payments will not even begin to foot the bill.

In the post-McNamara years (1981 on), World Bank policy has shifted away from poverty-alleviation. As one member of the new study-team expressed it, American taxpayers should not be asked to pay for "little experiments in so-called social progress" (230–231). The new pragmatism of the Bank includes an intention to suit projects to the recipient nations' policies, thus insuring more cooperation but doing less "modeling."

Yet as Robert Ayers assesses the situation, there is too much need for poverty alleviation in the world for the Bank to move drastically away from its previous policy. Further he suggests that an alliance between World Bank resources and the grassroots experience of many private voluntary relief organizations might reduce some of the bureaucratic cumbersomeness of Bank operations in the future. That, of course, remains to be seen.

International Monetary Fund

The IMF was created, along with the World Bank, to prevent a lapse into the massive unemployment and economic chaos that accompanied the depression and World War II. Specifically, its role was to "provide temporary finance—temporary credit, short-term liquidity—meant to prevent nations from taking certain actions in response to temporary difficulties, actions that would be unnecessary and harmful to themselves and the rest of the world" (Helleiner 43). Basically the IMF provides temporary aid to countries in temporary trouble so that they do not have to cut imports.

Obviously, as time has gone on, nations of the third world have needed this service more often than more developed member nations. For this reason, the Fund established Special Drawing Rights (SDRs) for poor nations that require automatic funding in the face of emergency. But there are some problems with this. The level of Special Drawing Rights has been static since January 1981, while the needs of poor nations have risen. In addition, the business of providing balance-of-payments credit to nations in trouble has increasingly been taken over by commercial banks. The poorest countries do not qualify for these loans because they are not credit-worthy. Although the World Bank has been doing more "structural adjustment lending," thus making further assistance in non-project aid available to poor countries, it is not enough to take care of the problem. In addition, such loans could compromise the Bank's emphasis on development in the long run (both in terms of diminished resources and divided focus).

A further problem involves the effect that the IMF, not a development agency, has on development programs and strategies. IMF policy has been strongly influenced by neo-classical economics. The conditions of their loans favor monetarist macroeconomic policies which focus on money supply, exchange rates, price stabilization, and balance of payments, to the detriment of other development objectives such as income distribution, human capital formation, and alleviation of poverty. Thus, IMF policy prescribes financial stabilization programs that often require cuts in public spending, including subsidies for basic consumer goods, social spending, and wages. This has consequences for the distribution of income that go far beyond the original purpose of the loans (David 19–20).

It is true that IMF provides only 10 percent of the money that goes into liquidity lending at present, but it is also true that their lending conditions have been accepted by a number of private banks and industrial lenders and that they have become a kind of global credit agency. Countries which do not fare well under IMF critieria are judged by private lenders to be unworthy of credit.

Thus it has an influence larger than its means and often promotes economic efficiency at the expense of basic needs efforts.

Multinational Corporations

In December 1974, ECOSOC of the United Nations established an Intergovernmental Commission on Transnational Corporations (1) to furnish a forum within the U.N. to discuss the phenomenon, (2) to promote an exchange of views about multinationals among governments, between businesses, and between labor and consumers, (3) to assist ECOSOC to develop a code of conduct for multinationals, and (4) to develop a comprehensive information system. Why was this necessary? What do these corporations represent that requires they be watched and controlled beyond measures adopted by individual nations to regulate business operations within their own borders?

The answer is easy. They represent centralized wealth and power that often threatens to exceed that of the very nations they occupy. Comparing the earnings of key multinational corporations (corporations that have operations in several countries) with the gross national products of nation-states indicates that in 1980 Exxon's profits were in excess of $100 billion, which is more than the entire GNP of Sweden and certainly of a whole host of third world nations. As Richard Barnet and Ronald Muller conclude:

> In the process of developing a new world, the managers of firms like General Motors, IBM, Pepsico, General Electric, Pfizer, Shell, Volkswagen, Exxon, and a few hundred others are making daily business decisions which have more impact than those of most sovereign governments on where people live; what work, if any, they will do; what they will eat, drink, and wear; what sorts of knowledge schools and universities will encourage; and what kind of society their children will inherit. (15)

The U.N. needs to study multinationals because they may well be one of the most powerful transnational forces in the world today. We need to study them because of the claims they make about being agents of positive change. Their basic credo is that growth promotes development. If profits are increased, prosperity will "trickle down" to those on the bottom of the economic scale. They promise peace and abundance through economic interdependence and the maximization of profit. But is that happening in the underdeveloped world where global corporations have had subsidiary companies for several decades?

It is quite true that global corporations facilitate the flow of goods, capital and advanced technology around the world. They employ hundreds of thousands of workers, often paying more than the prevailing wage of indigenous companies. They are eagerly sought by host nations, and their cultural influence in those nations is readily observable. They are clearly agents of change! But to discern the value of that change, let's assess their major claims to progress in the third world.

Global corporations claim to be a source of capital for underdeveloped nations, nations which desperately need capital for infrastructure and development projects. A very basic question to pose against this claim is whether such corporations bring more capital into their host countries than they take out. A United Nations study of global corporations operating in Latin America revealed some interesting facts about the financing of foreign subsidiaries of global corporations. During the years from 1957–1965, 83 percent of the funding for global corporations was local, indigenous to the host country. This included local banks, private local investors and reinvested earnings. According to the same study, between 1960 and 1968, U.S.-based global corporations reported taking an average of 79 percent of their net profits out of Latin America. Between 1965 and 1968, 82 percent of all profits of U.S. subsidiary manufacturing companies went to shareholders in the U.S. That means that for every dollar of profit, 52 cents left the country, even though 78 percent of the investment funds came from local sources. (Barnet 153–154)

Further problems are created by the fact that global corporations often use profits that stay within the host country to purchase local businesses, thus increasing the amount of profit that can be repatriated. Managers of such corporations assert that global businesses are more efficient than local operations—they can marshal more resources and apply more advanced technology to the production process. In addition, they claim that repatriating earnings to stockholders in the U.S. is preferable to transferring them to private bank accounts in Switzerland which is what local managers often do.

Nonetheless, the scale of global corporations, their monopolistic control of prices, and their political clout permits them to skirt efforts on the part of host countries to control the industrial sector and thus diminishes whatever advances in efficiency they offer. Parent companies in first world countries who trade with their own subsidiaries in third world countries can manipulate import and export prices so that "unfavorable" tariffs and taxes are minimized. And by reporting lower-than-accurate profit figures to the host governments, companies can avoid limitations placed on repatriation of earnings.

A second claim of global corporations is that they transfer valuable technology to underdeveloped countries. Certainly, technology is transferred through industrial enterprises, but the effect is often minimized by the lack of employee training, by the capital-intensive nature of first world technology, and by restrictions on the use of technology for local manufacturing. In addition, the technology offered is often that for "enhancing private consumption, not for solving social problems" (166).

Finally global corporations claim to be "educating for progress" by their advertising campaigns and by making first world media available to third world peoples. It is true that through TV, films, comic books, and billboards, U.S. corporations exert more control over Mexican youth than their own government or educational system. But is this a cultivation of taste? In a certain Peruvian village, young people were seen carrying stones painted to look like transistor radios because they could not afford the real thing, but knew that even the semblance of possession was a status symbol (Barnet 177). When malnourished children crave white bread and Pepsi over tortillas and milk, one has to question the value system being exported.

Lest all of this sound hopeless, Barnet offers possibilities and premonitions of change. Business thrives on competition, and it may be competition itself that controls the global corporations and forces them to comply with the desires and needs of host countries. Host countries are learning to change patent laws, to limit repatriation of profits, to restrict foreign banks, and to diversify their sources of industry and their trading partners. They are able to do this because German and Japanese companies are now competing with U.S. corporations for plant locations with resources and cheap labor. Deals can be negotiated where the most accommodating company wins. Economic ministry officials from poor countries are starting to compare notes and to make uniform demands. Third world governments are starting to investigate the pricing and profit practices of global corporations and to make it harder for them to manipulate evidence. Regional coalitions such as the Andean Common Market are starting to collect their own statistics and are no longer dependent on U.S. Department of Commerce statistics. If the poor host nations have learned anything from OPEC's negotiations with the energy-intensive first world nations, interdependence may well turn out to be a word that has more than rhetorical significance.

International Non-Governmental Organizations (INGOs)

The Red Cross

There are many INGOs that could be discussed here. We have selected two that have a humanitarian base and that illustrate the ways such organizations work to bind people together beyond national interests. The Red Cross was first established to care for wounded victims of the Napoleonic wars. Henri Dunant saw the suffering of the wounded and felt that their needs placed them beyond national war interests. He petitioned for the political neutrality of the wounded, of their physicians, and of their nurses, and he envisioned the creation of European Aid Societies in all European countries. He also envisioned that these societies could render service at the time of floods, fires and other catastrophes. The Geneva Convention of 1864 marked the first multilateral meeting of what was by then called the Red Cross. The structure agreed upon included the International Committee of the Red Cross which visits prisoners in war camps, and provides relief, mail, and information for relatives of prisoners; the League of Red Cross Societies, which promotes new societies, encourages cooperation among societies, develops Red Cross resources and services, and coordinates relief work; and national societies. Every four years an International Red Cross Conference convenes all three branches.

Over the years there has been tension between national societies which often reflect the political biases and policies of their individual governments and international branches of the society which tend to act more unilaterally, in accord with the expressed ideology of the society itself. Thus the tension between tribe and universal value asserts itself once again.

Amnesty International

Amnesty International is an INGO that acts on behalf of prisoners of conscience throughout the world. It has 2,500 organized groups in 140 countries, and works with a budget of more than $4 million.

Amnesty was founded in 1961 by Peter Benenson, a Catholic lawyer of Jewish descent. He had been defense counsel for many political prisoners and was one of the founding members of Justice, a group of lawyers campaigning for observation of the U.N. Declaration on Human Rights.

In 1960 he read of two Portuguese students who were sentenced to seven years of prison for drinking a public toast to freedom. He conceived the idea that bombarding the Salzac regime with letters of protest might be successful in securing their release. With others, he declared 1961 a year of "Appeal for Amnesty." The support he received for the idea led to a permanent organization, one that focused on letter writing, visits to prisoners, and support for prisoners' families.

Participating groups adopt specific "prisoners of conscience" whose cases are researched for them by an efficient research department. Prisoners who use violent methods of protest are eliminated from the protest lists, but the organization petitions for fair and prompt trials for all political prisoners and opposes the death penalty on behalf of all prisoners.

There is a yearly International Council where 200 delegates from national societies meet to discuss policy and progress. Members of the U.N. and the Red Cross are invited.

Private Voluntary Organizations

Again, one cannot possibly do justice to the large number of private development organizations that exist at the present time. What we are presenting here is a sampling of some of the most widely known. We are identifying their foci and methods of operation and including their addresses should you wish further information on them.

- *American Friends Service Committee* (1501 Cherry St., Philadelphia, PA 19102).

  This organization focuses on issues of peace and social justice, operating programs in many third world countries. Applicants for volunteer service should have development experience and administrative skills. The annual budget is $16 million.
- *American Jewish Joint Distribution Committee* (60 E. 42nd St., Suite 1914, New York, NY 10165).

  This organization aids Jewish communities throughout the world, operating a wide range of health, welfare and rehabilitation programs. It offers overseas employment. The annual budget is $40 million.
- *Bread for the World* (802 Rhode Island Ave., N.E., Washington, DC 20018).

  This is a Christian citizen's movement, dedicated to education about poverty and to influencing U.S. policy toward the end of hunger. Members are organized by political districts; they are expected to study poverty issues and to lobby congresspersons in the name of the hungry. The annual budget is $2.5 million.
- *CARE* (660 First Ave., New York, NY 10016).

  This organization focuses on feeding programs for school and pre-school children. It is also active in other basic needs projects—housing, nutrition, health care, water supply. It operates programs in 37 countries, in the poorest sections of the world. It offers career opportunities for service-oriented persons. The annual budget is $242.4 million.

■ *Catholic Relief Services* (1011 First Ave., New York, NY 10022).

CRS offers relief, welfare and self-help programs in many countries to aid refugees, war victims and other needy persons. Aid is strictly humanitarian and emphasis is on eventual self-sufficiency. Jobs are available in project planning, administration and analysis. The annual budget is $323.8 million.

■ *Christian Children's Fund* (Richmond, VA 23261).

Focus here is on meeting the needs of children through person-to-person assistance. It employs nationals and accepts no volunteers.

■ *Church World Service* (475 Riverside Drive, New York, NY 10115).

CWS is the relief, refugee resettlement and development agency of the National Council of Churches. Its projects involve local people and local fund raising. Emphasis is on supplying basic needs and community organization. Jobs are available for two year terms. Placements include Africa, Asia, and Latin America. The annual budget is $40 million.

■ *Ecumenical Development Cooperative Society* (475 Riverside Drive, New York, NY 10115).

EDCS is sometimes known as the churches' World Bank. Basically it provides an investment opportunity for persons interested in third world development. It makes low-interest long-term loans and technical assistance available to projects of the world's poor.

■ *Heifer Project International* (P.O. Box 808, 825 West Third St., Little Rock, AR 72203).

This organization supplies rural families in poor countries with livestock and training. The aim is to aid them in food specific projects, for one to three months. The annual budget is $5 million.

■ *Mennonite Central Committee* (Akron, PA 17501).

MCC places service-oriented volunteers in a variety of countries for work in agricultural development, nutrition, education, medical services, and other welfare projects. The annual budget is $25 million.

- *Opportunity International*—formerly the Institute for International Development, Inc. (IIDI) (P.O. Box 3695, Oak Brook, IL 60522).

    Opportunity International offers start-up or expansion loans to small business in third world countries. It has Partner Agencies in Latin America, Asia and Africa, has helped over 2,500 small businesses (through loans totaling over $2.6 million), and offers business management seminars and on-site consultation for recipients.

- *Overseas Education Fund* (2101 L St. N.W., Suite 916, Washington, DC 20037).

    This group aids indigenous organizations to develop and implement programs for improving the economic and social life of urban and rural poor. It is active in Central America, Nigeria, and Sri Lanka, among other places. Overseas jobs are available for indefinite periods of time.

- *Oxfam America* (115 Broadway, Boston, MA 02116).

    Oxfam funds local, grassroots projects in poor countries. It also works to inform policy makers and the general public about the root causes of poverty. The annual budget is $5 million.

- *Partnership for Productivity International* (2001 S St. N.W., Suite 610, Washington, DC 20009).

    This group aims to increase self-reliance in third world communities while respecting their cultural and social structures. Programs include education in credit, trade, investment, and computers. Overseas jobs are available. The annual budget is $4.5 million.

- *Save the Children Foundation, Inc.* (54 Wilton Rd., Westport, CT 06880).

    SCF has programs in thirty-eight countries. They are geared toward defending the rights of children and improving the quality of their lives. Thus the organization works with child sponsorship programs and with community development projects aimed at improving the environment. Overseas jobs are available. The annual budget is $40 million.

- *World Relief* (P.O. Box WRC, Wheaton, IL 60189).

  This is the relief, refugee resettlement, and development agency of the National Association of Evangelicals. Overseas jobs and volunteer positions are available. The annual budget is $15 million.

- *World Vision International* (919 W. Huntington Drive, Monrovia, CA 91016).

  This agency provides both emergency relief aid and programs of development among the rural poor in developing countries. Emphasis is placed on self-reliance, and projects develop basic human needs. Overseas jobs are available, as are a few intern positions. The annual budget is $100 million.

Obviously some international organizations are more accessible to the ordinary person than others. Yet the globally conscientious person needs to know about *all* types (from the United Nations to the Heifer Project) and to have well-informed opinions about their relative effectiveness. International organizations are taking action in the name of global peace and development every day. Some of them create a false sense of universalism by disguising selfish interests in the garb of altruistic motivations. Others operate to draw us out of our parochialism and into a mature awareness of our economic and political interdependence on one another. Study them, think about them, and decide where you can connect with what they offer.

BIBLIOGRAPHY

Archer, Clive. *International Organizations.* London: George Allen, 1983.

Ayers, Robert. *Banking on the Poor.* Cambridge: MIT Press, 1983.

Barnet, Richard J. and Ronald Muller. *Global Reach: The Power of the Multinational Corporations.* New York: Simon and Schuster, 1974.

Beckman, David, et al. *The Overseas List: Opportunities for Living and Working.* Minneapolis: Augsburg Publishing House, 1985.

Bennett, A.L. Ray. *International Organizations,* third edition. Englewood Cliffs: Prentice-Hall, 1984.

David, Wilfred L. *The IMF Policy Paradigm.* New York: Praeger, 1985.

Dunant, Henri. *The Origin of the Red Cross,* translated by Mrs. David H. Wright. Philadelphia: John C. Winston, 1911.

Forsythe, David P. *Humanitarian Politics: The International Committee of the Red Cross.* Baltimore: Johns Hopkins University Press, 1977.

Helleiner, Gerald. "The Rise and Decline of the International Monetary Fund," *Banking on Poverty: The Global Impact of the IMF and World Bank,* edited by Jill Torrie. Ontario: Between the Lines, 1983.

"International Organizations," *International Encyclopedia of the Social Sciences,* vol. 8. edited by David L. Sills. New York: The Macmillan Co. and The Free Press, 1968.

Power, Jonathan. *Amnesty International: The Human Rights Story.* New York: McGraw-Hill Book Co., 1981.

Pratt, R. Cranford. "International Bankers and the Crisis of Debt," *Banking on Poverty.*

The United Nations: A Handbook on the United Nations, edited by Moshe Sachs. New York: John Wiley and Sons, 1977.

Wells, Louis T. Jr. "The Multinational Business Enterprise: What Kind of International Organization?" *International Organization,* 25:447–464 (1971).

SUGGESTIONS FOR FURTHER STUDY

Barnet, Richard J. and Ronald Muller. *Global Reach: The Power of the Multinational Corporations.* New York: Simon and Schuster, 1974.

Evans, Peter. *Dependent Development: The Alliance of Multinational, State, and Local Capital in Brazil.* Princeton: Princeton University Press, 1980.

Simon, Arthur. *Bread for the World.* Grand Rapids: Eerdmans. 1984.

UNICEF News, any issue.

World Development Forum: A Twice-monthly Report of Facts,

Trends and Opinion in International Development. (Subscriptions available from: The Hunger Project, P.O. Box 789, San Francisco, CA 94101.)

DISCUSSION QUESTIONS AND ACTIVITIES

1. Discuss the following case: A woman who lives in your neighborhood has asked you to lend her a sum of money in order to attend classes at a local community college. You know that her husband does not approve of this venture, and will do all that he can to subvert her progress. What do you do?

   Can you relate your feelings and the conclusions you reached to the plight of ECOSOC, the World Bank, and many private organizations who must often decide whether or not to invest in development projects out of line with the policies of recipient nations?

2. Discuss the following case: A teacher in a Peruvian village can offer one night course to high school age students. Should he make that course a study of Andean music and folk stories which will develop a sense of pride in the people's Indian heritage? Or should he teach his students to speak English so that they can travel, study, and work in the larger "American" community?

3. In what ways has the corporate "consumer dream" diverted your attention and your money away from you own basic needs and into more "desirable" purchases? Keep a list during the week before your group meets, then share stories.

4. Read over the list of PVOs at the end of this chapter and pick the one that you would be most willing to work with. Share the reasons for your choices.

5. What is the most internationally mixed group that you have ever belonged to? What age were you at the time? What were the circumstances of your life? What positive things do you remember about the experience? What problems did the experience present for you? Record your memories and responses in your journals before the group meets. Then as you share these experiences, try to relate them to problems of international organization discussed in the chapter.

6. Read over your response journals and share pertinent entries.

8

Lobbying for National Responsibility

While much has been said in past chapters about the oppression of the poor, very little has been said about the oppression of the non-poor. This is especially interesting given the fact that in *Pedagogy of the Oppressed,* Paulo Freire states that "as the oppressed, fighting to be human, take away the oppressors' power to dominate and suppress, they restore to the oppressors the humanity they had lost in the exercise of oppression" (42). While there are obvious differences between the merely non-poor and the perpetrators of whom Freire speaks, members of developed nations must realize that by being part of the non-poor "culture of silence" they are participating in the continuation of poverty, and that that participation might well cost them a measure of their humanity.

The hope of this chapter is that, recognizing the truth of this statement, members of developed nations will rise above mute defense of the status quo and engage in political actions that promote mutual liberation.

Before this can occur, however, the non-poor must understand the source of their oppression. Among the various forces which enslave the non-poor, perhaps none is as debilitating as their feeling of personal inefficacy. Political scientists assure us that this is a major factor in why only 47 percent of eligible voters in the United States regularly vote in a major election (Lineberry 195), and marriage counselors confide that 60 percent of adults complain of "feelings of powerlessness" in their relationships.

Why is this the case? In the preface to his latest work, *Amusing Ourselves to Death,* Neil Postman asserts that we in the first world have come to love the very forces which oppress and enslave us (vi). Taking his cue from Aldous Huxley's *Brave New World,* Postman asserts that our oppression is not the product of some external tyrant, such as Orwell envisioned in *1984,* but is rather the result of our conscious or unconscious decision to relinquish the very freedoms which we hold dear. Why? Because freedom of thought and of will threaten to take us into difficult places. In response, we often prefer ignorance to hard truths and, to quote John Milton, "love Bondage more than Liberty, Bondage with ease than strenuous Liberty" (525). The danger in this is apparent. Such submission to the "given" forestalls the flourishing of human potential (leaving people at the lower stages of moral development, as described in Chapter One), and creates environments which encourage unethical behavior and lack of accountability.

By our acquiescence, we in the developed world give silent assent to the workings and policies of our governments, both moral and immoral. Our governments meanwhile effect policies which determine, in large part, the political and economic destinies of countries in the developing world. Through economic aid policies, through policies on agribusiness and multinational corporations, as well as through exported values such as consumerism, materialism and privatism, governments in the first world directly affect the well-being, or lack of same, of countries in the third world. All too often, military assistance to repressive regimes perpetuates the cycle of oppression and poverty.

Yet we, in our silence, are no less guilty than the governments which we inwardly condemn; what we do not choose to confront, we cannot privately damn. By our refusal to openly support appropriate economic assistance and to confront the unjust policies of our governments, we are guilty both of retarding the full development of ourselves and the full development of the poor. The purpose of this study is to propose ways in which concerned members of economically and politically powerful nations (specifically, the United States) might engage in political action which is both personally meaningful and responsive to the needs of those in the developing world.

The chapters in Part II present a number of factors that perpetuate endemic poverty in the world. They suggest ways in which first world nations have been part of the problem and they suggest ways in which first world nations can act to promote lasting, need-oriented economic development. Personal and group involvement in the political process can confront the former and promote the latter. But some practical knowledge of methodology is necessary.

Political Activism

Newcomers to the field of political activism often live under the false assumption that political action is only for great spiritual leaders like Gandhi or Martin Luther King Jr., or committed social radicals such as Abbie Hoffman or Jerry Rubin, little realizing that activism in the 1980's has been largely undertaken by middle-aged members of the middle class. The growing awareness that persons in the developing world are affected by decisions made on Capitol Hill, and of the importance of this fact, has led many "ordinary people" to lobby for greater national responsibility.

But on first entering the sometimes complex world of political activism, newcomers may be understandably bewildered by the multitudinous forms action can take, as well as by an unfamiliarity with the relative success of each form. For this reason we have composed a list of some of the kinds of social and political action, as well as an assessment of the strengths and weaknesses of each.

Voicing Concern

Implicit in the idea of representative government is the belief that governments are the servants of the public and therefore should conform national policy to public opinion. Obviously, this does not often occur. Indeed, governments often act with little regard for the concerns of the public, formulating and executing policies which cater to vocal, powerful or well organized special interest groups. Sometimes, however, governments respond with meritorious concern for the will of the people, enacting legislation which contributes to public betterment, and establishing standards of decency and respect for all citizens. The 19th Amendment and the Civil Rights Act of 1964 are tangible examples of ways in which the American government responded to the influence of its citizens. Justice, the need for both personal and global wholeness, requires that we exert influence upon our governments so that future foreign and domestic policy will be responsible.

The Vote

In "An Open Letter to North American Christians," the churches of Central America had this to say:

> If in the past you felt it to be your apostolic duty to send us missionaries and economic resources, today the frontier of your witness is within your own country. The conscious, intelligent and responsible use of your vote, the appeal to your representatives in the Congress, and the application of pressure by various means on your authorities can contribute to changing the course of our governments toward paths of greater justice and brotherhood or to accentuate a colonialist and oppressive policy over our people. (Wolterstorff 98)

One of the most overlooked and undermentioned, but most effective ways in which to lobby for national responsibility is to vote. While individuals as private citizens can occasionally have great influence in government, a more effective and reliable possibility is to vote for a congressperson whose values and voting record reflect a strong concern for justice. As mentioned earlier, less than half of eligible voters regularly vote, and "more than one fifth never participate in American politics in any way" (Lineberry 198). Feelings of inefficacy often prohibit people from exercising their right to have an opinion, but such feelings can be overcome by a conscious decision to act and, in acting, to help transform the world. Voter registration drives and dissemination of information to voters on candidates and issues are good ways to help people make that decision.

Letter-Writing

A good point of entrance into political activism, other than voting, is letter-writing. Along with voting, letter-writing is the staple of nearly two thirds of those who participate in American politics. (Only about 11 percent of those who are active in politics are what one would call "complete activists," meaning those who vigorously participate in all forms of political activity [Lineberry 195].) Yet many people regard the effectiveness of letter-writing with some suspicion. This suspicion is based on the assumption that congresspersons regularly receive large volumes of mail, and that personal letters are either discarded or have very little influence in decision or policy making. In their work *How You Can Influence Congress,* George Alderson and Everett Sentman include a statement from former congressman Jerome R. Waldie of California that runs directly counter to this claim. Waldie states: "There is no function more vital to a congressman than reading and replying to mail from back home. A congressman's constituents are literally his lifeblood" (41).

Few people realize how important personal letters of both support and opposition are to a congressperson. To a member of the House who must campaign for reelection every second year, these letters are a vital means of connection between the member and his or her constituents. For senators, who face reelection every six years, the need for constant feedback and criticism vis-à-vis letters is a little less important, though only slightly so. In general, legislators and their aides feel that a letter that is given swift attention and replied to promptly has the greatest potential for increasing a congressperson's appeal (42).

Letter-writing becomes even more important when one realizes that, contrary to popular opinion, many issues are decided by legislators who have received little or no mail on the subject (41). Thus it is very possible that a persuasive and well-argued letter from a single individual can make the difference in a legislator's decision.

Yet even people convinced of the value of such action fail to write to their legislators because they do not know how to go about writing them. Alderson and Sentman propose ten simple guidelines for writing a congressperson:

1. Make the letter a page or less, covering only one subject, written in your own words and including thoughts of your own.

2. When your letter concerns a bill already being considered in Congress, refer to the bill by its number and name, if you know them.

3. Tell the legislator exactly what you want him or her to do, and give your reasons for adopting this position. Stress, if possible, how the issue can affect people in your congressional district or state.

4. Ask the legislator to tell you his or her position on the matter: "Will you support this legislation?" or "Will you oppose this legislation?"

5. Show your awareness of the legislator's past actions. If possible, cite an instance of his or her recent voting on related issues.

6. Don't mention your membership in a citizens' organization. The individual citizen's letter is more influential than the letter obviously inspired by an organization.

7. Don't send in a form letter or preprinted postcard unless you absolutely can't take the time to write your own letter. (Form letters have $\frac{1}{10}$th the impact of a personal letter.)

8. Don't repeat slogans or phrases from a newsletter or form letter. *Your own words* will make the crucial difference.

9. If you don't know the names of your senator or congressperson, call the information desk of your local public library. Use these addresses:

Senator X   Congressman Y
U.S. Senate   or Congresswoman Z
Washington, D.C. 20510 House of Representatives
                             Washington, D.C. 20515

10. When your legislator replies, write a follow-up letter to reemphasize your position and give reactions to his/her response. Remember to make a copy of your original letter and keep it on file so that you will

recall what was said, and a reply may take several months. (53–54)

Writing more than once a month, a lobbyist runs the risk of being relegated to "pen-pal" status and, consequently, not taken seriously. Yet it is every citizen's constitutional right to contact his or her legislators and express personal views; therefore, no one should feel it necessary to apologize for doing so. Finally, unless a writer is furious with a particular legislator, it never hurts to make letters enjoyable to read. There is pitiful little wit disseminated in most government offices!

Visiting Washington

Another way to expand citizen influence, and a good follow-up to letter-writing, is to schedule a visit to Washington or to a legislator's state office for a face-to-face meeting. Yet newcomers as well as veterans to social/political activism are intimidated by the prospect of meeting their senators or congresspersons. They fear that their legislators, their most direct line of influence, are too busy to spend time with ordinary citizens and that they are generally disinterested in the social and political convictions of their constituents. While it is true that there are legislators who are deaf to their constituents, they are often remembered unfavorably by voters on election day (Alderson 91).

According to Alderson and Sentman newcomers should "act confident, even if they don't feel it. They probably know more than their representative does about a particular issue, because a legislator is a jack-of-all-trades" (91). Legislators are often fragmented in terms of specific issues; very few have the time needed to thoroughly study a single issue. Therefore when informed citizens meet their congresspersons, they have a decided advantage (and responsibility).

When presenting their case, lobbyists should do so in a firm but not antagonistic tone. They will usually be asked several difficult or provocative questions during the course of the presentation. It is not necessarily a sign that the congressperson is not on their side, but rather that he or she is trying to discern the extent of their commitment to and familiarity with the issue. Often such meetings are only five to ten minutes in duration; lobbyists should be brief and cover only the main points of the issue.

Finally, legislators should be listened to but not allowed to be evasive. If the legislator tries to evade the issue, it should be tactfully repeated and he or she pressed for a commitment. Legislators are experts at evasion and rhetoric; the best way to circumvent such tactics is to become familiar with them and always to press for a response. If the legislator is firmly opposed to a position, his or her reasons for that position can be solicited and carefully refuted. While these tactics may not sway a legislator's decision, they will at least leave him or her with the sense that his or her constituents are well informed, committed, and a force to be dealt with.

Lobbyists should not be surprised if they meet with an aide rather than the legislator. The aide is the congressperson's ears and eyes, is familiar witth the legislator's position, and should be treated with the same respectful insistence.

Organizing a Legislative Campaign

For extremely committed individuals a logical fourth step in gaining greater social control is the organization of a legislative campaign. The advantage here is that a well-organized group or campaign can achieve "results that you as an individual never could" (Alderson 109). While legislators are interested in the opinions of all of their constituents, they are especially interested in the opinions and positions of organized groups within their congressional district or state. The reasons for this are obvious. A well-organized group wields considerably more political influence than an individual because they have greater voting potential. If a legislator votes against an issue which is tenaciously held to by a group, he or she is at greater risk than if he or she voted against an issue held to by a fragmented and unorganized group of individuals. It is probably true that to legislators "organization" means the possibility of organized opposition or support, yet there is always the danger of individuals letting the group speak for them and not taking personal, direct action. (See #6 in the guidelines for writing a congressperson.)

How does one go about organizing a legislative campaign? In Chapter Ten we will explore the formation of "communities of commitment," one way in which individuals might get together to respond to one another's needs while simultaneously responding to the needs of the developing world. Likewise, organizing a legislative campaign can begin with individuals coming together around a shared concern for social, political and economic justice.

Once a group has been formed, attention to several key considerations will make the process of organization that much easier. First is the need to be clear about what the focus for the group is to be. Many well-intentioned organizations have degenerated into politically ineffectual forums for debate because its members had multiple agendas. At this stage groups need to take time to listen to every member's area of concern, but also to remember that a campaign focused on a specific issue is considerably more effective than one whose purpose is abstract or fragmented among several different issues. Speaking out for aid to refugees in a particular area of the world makes more sense than campaigning for refugees in general. The information necessary to present the case can be mastered and concrete actions proposed.

The next step is, of course, to plan the campaign. Here, the rule is "the more voices, the better the campaign." It is essential at this stage that every member of the group contribute to the tailoring of the campaign, for in activism, as in music, a single voice or a single musical theme monotonously repeated becomes flat and distasteful. In building and planning a campaign, legislative lobby groups need the creativity and resourcefulness of every one of its members—to assess possible sources of support, both physical and financial, in the local community; to discuss potential tactics and means of persuasion; to think about potential sources of opposition; and to conceive of every possible way to involve other members of the community.

Sample tactics include the three things mentioned previously, as well as mass petitions, newsletters, lobbying community leaders, and media exposure. (For a more exhaustive study of legislative campaigns and lobbying groups refer to Alderson and Sentman's *How You Can Influence Congress* and Marc Caplan's *Ralph Nader Presents a Citizen's Guide to Lobbying.*)

Showing Resolve

Parades and Marches

A second form that political activism can take is symbolic actions and gestures. Symbolic actions rely upon persons' physical presence and participation in actions which make visual statements. They do not, therefore, hinge upon an ability to articulate (verbally) opposition to or support for a particular position. If legislative groups and lobbying are more for the vocally inclined, demonstrations and civil disobedience are for the more dramatic. Let us take a closer look at various forms of symbolic action.

One of the most widely known forms of symbolic action is the march or parade, one which recalls the civil rights demonstrations of the late 1950's and early 1960's, the demonstrations of Iranian students in the U.S. in the mid to late 1970's, and caravans of Salvadoran refugees in the late 1980's. The way in which marches and parades differ is minor, but worth mentioning.

According to Gene Sharp, author of *The Politics of Non-Violent Protest,* a march is "a group of people walk[ing] in an organized manner to a particular place which is regarded as intrinsically significant to the issue involved" (152), while a parade differs only in that its point of termination is not "of intrinsic significance to the demonstration" (154). A group of people walking to a particular corporate center for the purpose of questioning its investments in South Africa is a march; CROP walks for the alleviation of hunger are parades. Both marches and parades, however, are most effective when they employ posters and banners, and the wide dissemination of leaflets supporting the group's particular position.

More important than making the group's views known to the general public, however, is gaining the attention and, hopefully, extensive coverage of the media. For example, on July 12, 1982, 550,000 concerned citizens gathered in New York's Central Park to support the United Nations Special Session on Disarmament and to call for a freeze and reduction of all nuclear weapons and a transfer of military budgets to human needs. The parade, because of its sheer size, deserved the media's attention, and the media affirmed the importance of the event by giving it front page coverage. Millions were influenced by the event who were nowhere near New York and who wouldn't have known about it had it not been for the attention of the media.

A somewhat more extreme example is that of the Iranian students who, during the hostage crisis of the late 1970's, marched through the streets of Washington, D.C. and, at the parade's end, burned an American flag in effigy. The media pounced on the event. Americans everywhere were stunned at the flagrant and brazen contempt of the small group of students for an important national symbol, an effect which would not have been possible without the support of the media.

From these examples one can see the importance of the media's role in determining the impact which an event such as a parade or a march will have on the rest of the world. What the media does not reveal is just as important as what it does disclose. For example, one can easily determine what a network's or newscaster's ideological bias is by what he or she chooses to show of a group's event on the evening news. If all the footage that the newscaster shows is shots of bored or angry participants, you can be pretty sure that he or she disapproves of the group's position and that the event will probably be remembered unfavorably. If, on the other hand, the newscaster shows footage of excited and peaceful-minded protesters, the group is more likely to attract the much sought-after emotional support of the public. The media can be a helpful force in spreading the message of the event or can be a manipulative force, distorting the event to suit public fascinations. Political action groups need to cultivate some media contacts that they can count on to be fair, and keep them well informed of activities.

Participation in a march or parade, aside from being an effective means of demonstrating support for, or opposition to, a specific issue, is often a bonding and empowering experience. The need to affirm the participants while at the same time affirming the importance of the issue is very real. Effective political action groups keep these two things in tension.

Boycotts

Concerned groups of citizens may expand their influence and reinforce their commitment to an issue by selective boycotts of certain goods, or certain manufacturers. Such actions can be undertaken for a variety of reasons: (1) the item or manufacturer may possess certain "immoral" qualities; (2) the item may not be available to all socio-economic groups; or (3) the boycotters may object to the manner in which the product was produced (e.g. cheap labor exacted from third world or migrant workers) or they may object to the way in which profits will be used (e.g. the diversion of profits to support unpopular or "immoral" groups or movements).

An example of a recent successful consumer's boycott involves the Nestlé Company and its subsidiaries (e.g. Stouffer's). In the early 1980's, the company came under the close scrutiny of political activists and concerned lobbying groups for its promotion of the sale of infant formula to developing countries. Infant formula was promoted without adequate instruction of consumers in the sanitary preparation of the product, as well as without sufficient thought given to the physical and economic constraints on bottle feeding (e.g. lack of safe water, inability to purchase the formula once a free sample had been used up) in contrast to the greater appropriateness of breast feeding. As a result of their attempt to export an inappropriate product to the third world, the Nestlé Company was publicly denounced. Pressure from boycotters eventually forced Nestlé to make substantial changes in their advertising of infant formula.

When dealing with large corporations, activists should remember that the opposition is often a group's most effective and important tool. Careful use of the opposition's own statements to reveal its position can be the most effective way of bringing down an industrial Goliath. It can also lead to the exposure of some fairly humorous pomposities. (A consumers' boycott, or any other form of political activism, for that matter, need not always be serious and self-important. A tactic that is not at least occasionally enjoyable is a poorly chosen tactic [Alinsky 128].)

Engaging in a consumers' boycott has some of the greatest potential for first world identification with the third world, for not only does it remind the participants what deprivation feels like, it calls into question the need for consumer goods in the face of more appropriate and cost-effective ones. Part of becoming a whole human being is not only what you willingly embrace and identify with, but also what you refuse to be enslaved by.

Non-Violent Demonstrations

A more dramatic but equally effective way of achieving a group's ends is to periodically engage in non-violent, non-cooperative activities such as sit-ins, sit-downs, or any of the various other "ins" which a group may wish to employ. Such actions require a high degree of commitment to an issue, an awareness of the legal consequences of chosen actions, and chutzpah. While these actions are certainly not for everyone, participation in them can be liberating.

The objective of a sit-in, according to Gene Sharp, is to "disrupt the normal pattern of activities" in a particularly significant building (371). The occupation of the facility by the demonstrators may either be spontaneous or planned, and for either a definite or indefinite period of time. To many, such tactics sound extremist, but that many companies now equip their new facilities with specially designated areas for sit-ins and other demonstrations (they are, of course, placed in areas where the protesters will have little visibility and little possibility of interference) is a testimony to their integration into the political process.

Clayborne Carson speaks of the very real psychological effect of sit-ins on young black students in the 1960's, stating that "as local white leaders gave in to the student demands, an increasingly self-confident, able, and resourceful group of young black activists emerged as spokespersons for the local protest movements" (18). Certainly, no one will dispute the effects produced on both the British colonists and the Indian peasants alike by Gandhi's organization of massive demonstrations by the poor. And students of the 1980's are beginning to find their political voice through sit-ins demanding explanation of their administrations' investments in South Africa.

Slightly different from the sit-in is the sit-down, where resisters actually sit down in an area to impede or obstruct the flow of business or traffic. In the sit-in the goal is often to establish a new pattern, as in the civil rights movement, to open up a restricted area to previously excluded persons, whereas the goal of the sit-down is to physically interfere in the normal operation of a place. Sit-downs are therefore somewhat more provocative in that they are attempts to confuse, disarm and aggravate the opponent. Gandhi's workers' strikes qualify here.

One of the most astonishing examples of the success of sit-downs, however, comes from World War II, during Hitler's attempted occupation of Norway. Members of a small village, led by a Protestant pastor, sat down on the railroad ties and refused to allow the Nazis to enter the village. When the soldiers realized that the only way they were going to occupy the village was to run over the villagers, they refused and returned home. While it is unlikely that your group will ever face such extreme circumstances, actions such as this one build a group's confidence and encourage members to believe that, through perseverance, changes can be made.

Creative groups may occasionally wish to adopt other means of influencing the government. Religious communities, for example, may find a pray-in or a fast more appropriate than more typical means of political action. College or university professors, as well as high school teachers, may register their political opinions vis-à-vis a teach-in.

Saul Alinsky relates a humorous example of a type of "in" which his group threatened to employ in order to get the city government of Chicago to improve the living conditions of blacks in a sub-standard area of the city. Alinsky and his co-workers decided upon O'Hare airport as the target for their action. If the plan had been activated, members of Alinsky's Woodlawn Organization would have gone to the airport, armed only with books and newspapers, and occupied all of the stalls in the men's and ladies' rooms. When one considers that O'Hare is one of the busiest airports in the world, the consequences of having every toilet "taken" boggles the mind. Indeed, when the threat of this action was passed on to the administration, Alinsky and his members found themselves in conference with the powers-that-be the next day.

The "content" of your political action is not for anyone else to decide. You may find that human rights issues are more pressing than issues of economic aid. Others may feel that U.S. compliance with United Nations guidelines on refugees or government restrictions on international business demand their political energies. U.S. policies in relation to a particular third world country may absorb your study and your action. Lobbying for better education about the third world in public schools and for programs to train health care workers in the field would appeal to parents' or teachers' groups. (Bread for the World and IMPACT, addresses given in Chapter Ten, are two agencies that collect and disseminate information on legislation and policy that relate to justice and hunger issues.) What we have given you are methodologies to implement your concerns, and hopefully a reason for taking action. To refuse to do so is to risk enslavement by apathy and the replacement of courage and democracy with cowardice and determinism.

BIBLIOGRAPHY

Alderson, George and Everett Sentman. *How You Can Influence Congress.* New York: E.P. Dutton, 1979.

Alinsky, Saul D. *Rules for Radicals.* New York: Random House, 1972.

Carson, Clayborne. *In Struggle: SNCC and the Black Awakening of the 1960s.* Cambridge: Harvard University Press, 1981.

Freire, Paulo. *Pedagogy of the Oppressed,* translated by Myra Ramos. New York: Continuum, 1970.

King, Martin Luther, Jr. *A Testament of Hope: The Essential Writings of Martin Luther King, Jr.,* edited by James Melvin Washington. San Francisco: Harper and Row, 1986.

Lineberry, Robert L. *Government in America: People, Politics, and Policy.* Boston: Little, Brown and Company, 1986.

Milton, John. *The Complete Poetical Works of John Milton,* edited by Douglas Bush. Boston: Houghton Mifflin, 1965.

Postman, Neil. *Amusing Ourselves to Death: Public Discourse in the Age of Showbusiness.* New York: Viking, 1985.

Sharp, Gene. *The Politics of Non-Violent Action.* Boston: Porter-Sargent, 1974.

Wolterstorff, Nicholas. *Until Justice and Peace Embrace.* Grand Rapids, Michigan: Eerdmans, 1983.

SUGGESTIONS FOR FURTHER STUDY

Alderson, George, and Everett Sentman. *How You Can Influence Congress.* New York: E.P. Dutton, 1979.

Caplan, Marc. *Ralph Nader Presents a Citizen's Guide to Lobbying.* New York: Dembner Books, 1983.

Gandhi, M.K. *Non-Violent Resistance.* New York: Schocken Books, 1951.

Hessel, Dieter T. *A Social Action Primer.* Philadelphia: The Westminster Press, 1972.

McFarland, Andrew S. *Common Cause: Lobbying in the Public Interest.* Chatham, New Jersey: Chatham House Publishers, 1984.

DISCUSSION QUESTIONS AND ACTIVITIES

1. Do you consider yourselves to be political people? The answer may well vary from person to person. If you are, what motivates you? If you are not, what have been your fears of the political arena?

2. What do you remember about the political activism of the 1960's? In your estimation were the movements of this decade significant in changing U.S. domestic and foreign policy? If so, how?

3. Pick an issue that concerns most of you and a congressperson known to all of you. Then role-play a discussion on this issue between a concerned voter and the chosen legislator. When the role-play is over, critique the methodology of each participant.

4. The week before your group meets to discuss this chapter, spend time each day with the newspaper, cutting out articles that have to do with U.S. policy and actions in the third world—from articles on third world debt to U.S. banks, to articles on military/diplomatic intervention in unstable regions. Each of you pick one article to present. Then as a group decide

what kind of response/action a concerned person or group of persons might take in the face of this issue.

5. Having read what you have read so far, try to project as a group what you think the global issues of the 1990's are going to be. Is there any way that you can be in dialogue with your elected representatives about these issues *now,* asking questions and provoking thought?

6. Read over your response journals. If there are some items there that have not yet surfaced, share them.

9

Living Responsibly

Chapter Eight discusses concrete political actions that a person or group of persons can use to express their concerns for global justice. This chapter talks about *lifestyles, attitudes* toward the poor, and the relationship between the two.

Empowering the Poor

The epigram for Basic Needs International, a development education organization, is "Meeting basic needs is a matter of justice" (not charity). Quite simply this means that every person *deserves* to have access to food, clean water, education, health care, and work that provides sufficient income to support these needs. The world has sufficient resources for this to take place, but as we have been discussing throughout, gross discrepancies of income among countries and between elites and peasants within developing countries keep this from happening. The goal of economic aid and legislative changes is not to provide a global welfare system that "takes care" of the poor (charity). This mentality would, in a short time, send us right back to paternalistic colonialism. Rather, the goal is to empower the poor—to admit, in all humility, that the poor often know what they need and how to get it, but the means of production are not available to them. It is our role in the developed world to see that opportunities for self-development are available to the third world poor and that their movement toward self-reliance takes place in a supportive environment (justice).

An interesting story is told of St. Francis. A brother had piously claimed that "his compassion [for a poor man] was changed to heart-felt affection," to which Francis replied, "Brother, it is true that he is a poor man, but there is perhaps no one in the whole region richer than he is in desire." After this, Francis commanded the brother to ask the poor man's pardon and to beg him to pray for him (Boff 24). Faithful response to the poor is more than compassion; it is a recognition of their riches and a desire to participate in the liberation of their potential. It is also a willingness to learn from and be guided by their experience of the world which often involves an endurance and industriousness we know little about.

Denis Goulet describes the liberation of the poor as "a victory over privilege, stagnation and dependency" (555). It involves freedom from the psychic paralysis that results from internalizing images of inferiority, from political and economic constraints which block a people's creativity, and from servitude to nature and ignorance. The goal is "to transform hitherto passive human beings into active subjects creating their own history" (556). In Goulet's view, economic development cannot take place unless the poor are emancipated from their fears and restraints and liberated to the creative solving of their own problems through means appropriate to their conditions.

We often talk about resources as if they were all mineable and measurable, and we forget that any country's greatest resource is its people. Yet, people remain a latent resource "until they are stirred into action by a pedagogy which gives them pride in their own values, shows them how these values can arm them with tools for acting effectively in their concrete surroundings, and welds them into strong community networks of mutual supports in the fact of obstacles and failures" (560). Such a revolutionary approach to learning has been proposed by Paulo Freire, a Brazilian educator, and demonstrated in several Latin American communities. It is an approach that causes the poor to assess their own situation, to discuss it, and to become articulate about their needs. It gives them the perspective and the literacy tools they need to take charge of their own lives.

Freire begins his book *Pedagogy of the Oppressed* (quoted in Chapter Eight) with a critical assessment of traditional education, what he calls the "banking" method. Here the teacher possesses all of the "goods" and deposits them in the students' minds, from which they can be retrieved in kind. Thus, the values of the educator are transferred intact, and the student is "colonized." The truth is necessarily compromised because new ideas in the words of the "colonizer" are directionless.

Freire's pedagogy, on the other hand, was designed not to invest ideas in students' minds but to liberate ideas taking shape there. It was designed to enable illiterate adults to think, read and write simultaneously by having them generate their own vocabulary. They would begin by discussing a picture of life as they experience it. Out of these discussions the teacher would extract key words, combine the consonants in these words with a whole range of vowels, have the learners sound out the new syllables and then create words from them. Thus *campesinos,* or peasants, were learning to read words which expressed their own consciousness and, through this process, to understand and articulate their own needs and plans. This was truly education for self-discovery and self-development.

A good case study to illustrate the points made so far is provided by SEWA (Self-Employed Women's Association of Admedabad), founded in India in 1972. The participating women are street vendors, artisans, junksmiths and garment makers. They banded together to find a way of combating coerced payments to money lenders and bribes to policemen, as well as the general disdain of the public. They now have their own bank with 1,000 shareholders and 10,000 depositors. They have become educated in self-help economics and have provided health services, maternity and widow's benefits for their membership. (561)

Another case study comes from the Quechua communities of Bolivia where producer cooperatives have been formed for ceramic and rug artisans. The purpose of the cooperatives is to diversify sources of income for these rural Indian peoples in a manner that will revitalize Quechua culture and hand-work traditions. They have insisted on using "appropriate" technologies for their operations, those which are in harmony with ancient Quechua habits and which can be shared by all in the community. This has meant that they have rejected electric kilns for their ceramic cooperative, in that all in the village can not afford electricity, and they have gone to kerosene ovens. By group decision the surplus from cooperative endeavors goes to all members of the village, whether they are members of the cooperatives or not. Cultural and economic needs are being met simultaneously and indigenously.

Empowerment of the poor to solve their own problems has also been effective in the area of health services. Emanuel de Kadt credits a good bit of the energy for and success of cooperative community health services to Paulo Freire's pedagogy of the oppressed which is sometimes described by the term *conscientization* (helping the poor and exploited "to become conscious of their situation"). In many poor areas of the world the residents have become acutely aware of the need for preventive health programs that call for their active participation.

Successful projects include a people's pharmacy in Lima's Villa el Salvador, built in 1980; programs of community health services, both preventive and curative, in Cuba and Nicaragua; and the "Hospital Without Walls" in San Ramen, Costa Rica, which expanded its commitment beyond health care to improvements in land tenure and physical infrastructure. In Asia and Africa, community health workers have been used to implement extensive programs in both curative and preventive health care (including sanitation, clean water supply, and communicative disease control). In Latin America, community health workers tend to be more hedged in by physicians, but still do much in the areas of promotion of health education and prevention of disease. In all places, community health workers can be the link between traditional means of treating disease and modern medical technology, because they come from among the people themselves.

With all that has been said in Chapters Five and Six about international and domestic constraints on poverty-oriented programs, this discussion of empowerment of the poor may sound naive—a good idea that does not have a chance except in isolated incidents. But, in fact, there are more "people" than financiers, corporate heads, and government officials, and it is just possible that a new international economic order will come—can only come—from the bottom up. As de Kadt argues, "it is wrong to assume that governments are monolithic. Within any large state bureaucracy there are always nooks and crannies where an orientation can operate which is more progressive . . . than the dominant government line" (580). Goulet agrees that "even an authoritative government like that found in Brazil can tolerate a considerable degree of participation in local problem-solving" (565), because of diversified regional priorities. We talked about farmers' associations in Chapter Six which could lobby for fair food pricing. Religious communities in many developing countries are talking about the utilization of spiritual power to address systemic problems of the poor. Co-ops and community health systems have been mentioned in this chapter. All of these things are already in process to some degree. It is our job as conscientious outsiders to support them through selected international organizations, through political lobbying for supportive aid, and, perhaps, through empowering ourselves to live outside the entrapments of first world consumerism.

The Simple Lifestyle: St. Francis

When people speak of the simple lifestyle they often either imagine "quaint" folks like the Amish or "weirdos" like the 1960's hippies. Surely we could learn much from both groups if we took the time to study their communalism. But fighting consumerism can also be an attitude, an attitude that encompasses a refusal to be forced to want what the media tells us to want and a consciousness of how our lifestyles contrast with and impinge on the underdeveloped world.

This attitude has probably never been as clearly articulated as it was in the life of St. Francis of Assisi. In writing about the liberating aspects of St. Francis' life, Leonardo Boff makes this comparison of our age to his message:

> The crisis that we are suffering is structural in nature and concerns the basics of our system of life together. This is the reason for its dramatic and undeniable character. The crisis of the global system derives from the crisis specific to the ruling class, the bourgeois class that has directed our history for the past five centuries. . . . We find ourselves at the end of one era and at the beginning of a new one. Within this context, the figure of Francis is a highly appealing one. (4–5)

Boff finds St. Francis to be a fascinating example for the modern age because he rebelled *against* the main currents of the western culture, while being very much a product *of* the western tradition. In his day, Francis found a way of articulating the human heart, which was under suspicion by his culture and official Christianity, and he articulated it from within the church and on the basis of an European education. His biography makes this paradox clear.

Francis was born to a rich bourgeois textile merchant and his wife. He led an early life as a "bohemian minstrel" and later took his father's place in the marketplace. A severe illness brought him close to death and changed his attitude to life. After this point, he felt a strong affinity for the poor and began giving away his profits to the poor. Finally, during a dispute with his father over business, he stripped off all of his clothing, renounced the privileges of money, and sought refuge in the arms of a bishop who happened to be present. This was his entry into holy orders. He lived for three years as a hermit and then for many years lived and worked among the lepers, completely identifying with their material and social poverty.

Francis has come to be identified with both poverty and with a reverence for life. He saw possessions as obstacles to be overcome in the realization of living community (a connection with all things), so it is quite easy to see him as Boff does, as an ally of modern ideologies that speak of a preferential option for the poor.

Poverty is not an accident of nature; it results from "definite economic, social and political situations and structures" (50). The poor fear the power of the rich to exploit and abuse them; the rich fear the vindictive rebellion of the poor. So each views the other suspiciously and defensively. The greatness of St. Francis, once a prosperous bourgeois merchant, "consisted in seeing the poor with the eyes of the poor, allowing him, thereby, to discover the value of the poor" (50).

What does it mean to identify with the poor—or to opt for the poor? It means, in part, adopting an anti-consumerist stance in a consumer-oriented world. It means participating in the struggles of the poor in such a way that their opportunities to grow and their sense of self-worth expands. It means "humanization through fraternity," recognizing always that while poverty is a manifestation of evil and injustice, choosing to identify with the poor is a manifestation of solidarity and brotherhood. [This contrast is made clear in the chart contrasting "living poorly" with "living responsibly."]

As Boff describes this momentum in the life of Francis, "It is precisely toward the periphery [the marginalized] that Francis directs himself. From the periphery he begins to converge on the center [of his culture], calling all to conversion" (114). This is a pilgrimage that many conscientious persons in developed countries are choosing for themselves—to turn toward the problem, to read about, visit and get involved in dignity-promoting projects in the third world, then to "return home" disturbed—disturbed about foreign policy, about aid policy and about the way we live in the rich nations. As Boff contends, a contact with Francis, or with the Francis journey, brings "crisis" that invites practice. Practice may be involvement in international work; it may be involvement in political action; it may also be trying to live responsibly, simply, in a grossly overmaterialized environment.

Living the Simpler Life

Let's look at why and how some folks have tried to do this. First of all, what is the problem that living simply hopes to address? The American Friends Service Committees publishes the following "myth" of consumer discrepancies: "If the world were a global village of one hundred people, five of them would be [North] Americans. These five would have one third of the village's income, and the other ninety-five would subsist on the rest." (4) One might well argue that, as a result of the consolidation of wealth, consumerism has become so pervasive in our culture that it has defined who we are. We use the purchase of material objects to signal our success, win the "right kind" of friends, and to make ourselves feel good if other things are not going well in our lives. At the same time that we are seeking our own well-being through acquisition of fashionable objects and services, our economic objectives have little regard for the actual quality of life: "Official U.S. economic policy does not care about what consumption choices are available to us, only about the total level of consumption. . . .

Auto accident costs, including hospital and funeral bills, raise the Gross National Product (GNP) and are considered signs of economic health." (19)

People who advocate living responsibly or living more simply want both to be free of the consumer trap (to be in charge of their own lives) and to do economic justice (empowering the poor to change their lives). This means lobbying for fair import-export agreements, supporting the small family farm and calling for a cutback in large-farm agribusiness, supporting foreign aid for basic needs, and lobbying for an end to escalating arms sales. It means calling for energy-efficient transportation systems in U.S. cities, cooking simple nutritional meals, cutting down on purchase of appliances, recycling whatever materials can be recycled, and using a minimum of non-recyclable goods. It means living in one's personal and family life the way we wish rich nations would live, thus reinforcing our own values and commitments, and hopefully providing a consciousness-raising model.

Food

One of the largest areas to be addressed in the effort to live responsibly is food consumption. One of the first steps toward a responsible attitude toward food is to disabuse oneself of simplistic diagnoses of the problem of hunger. As we have already discussed, global malnutrition is not a matter of the availability of food but of its distribution and economic accessibility. Let's look at a few comparative cases. China has one half the cultivated acreage per person of India, yet in twenty-five years China has made considerable strides toward the elimination of acute malnutrition. In Mexico, much of the rural population suffers from malnourishment, while in Cuba, which has less cultivated land per person, the people are sufficiently fed.

A second step is to become aware of legislative actions that control food aid and to express an opinion about how U.S. dollars are spent. Having researched the field, the American Friends Service Committee concludes: "The best aid that we in the United States can give is to oppose corporate control and U.S. military and economic 'aid' that distorts the growth and distribution of

Living Poorly Means . . .	_Living Responsibly Can Create . . ._
Inferior and non-nutritious food sold through stores that often charge more than they do in affluent areas.	Neighborhood food cooperatives, farmers markets, and cooperative urban gardens that operate on a non-profit basis.
Risk of eviction when rent or mortgage money isn't available, when a government agency plans a new highway, or as a result of rising prices and "gentrification." Risk of arson, if your building costs the landlord too much to maintain.	Neighborhood associations, urban and rural land trusts, and housing cooperatives responsive to and often owned by residents.
Almost total dependence on expensive experts or your own skills for repairs, maintenance work, or home improvements.	The opportunity to share and barter time and skills with neighbors and community members.
Fear of rape, robbery, burglary, murder, and other crimes of violence.	Neighborhood safety organizations where members of the community cooperate to minimize violence.
Isolation, hopelessness, and loneliness after "retirement."	Friendship, intellectual contact, and important roles to play in the community.
Fear of arbitrary and unexpected layoffs and firings.	Job protection through union membership, cooperatively run workplaces, and collectively owned businesses.
Dependence on impersonal, centralized agencies and expensive physicians for health care.	Locally controlled, responsive health-care facilities and personal knowledge about how to keep healthy.
Vulnerability to environmentally caused disease (black lung, cancer, emphysema) and to increased costs and dangers from environmental hazards (acid rain, chemical wastes, nuclear accidents).	Life in an environment that is free of the fear of unnatural diseases and disasters.
Unemployment, hopelessness, fear, drug use, and crime among young people.	Self-help housing, gardening, and skills-oriented projects that help young people do something for themselves, their neighborhoods, and their towns.
Garbage-filled streets, yards, and lives.	Recycling projects that clean up neighborhoods and yield profits for the community.
Dependence on centralized sources for heat, electricity, and other basic utilities.	Solar energy systems and other renewable, locally controlled energy sources.
Payment of high prices for advertising, profits, and transport of goods thousands of miles.	An emphasis on locally produced goods, services, and skills.
Reductions in employment and social services due to militarism and unequal resource distribution.	A secure, nonviolent world where basic material needs are met for all without the threat or reality of war.

(American Friends Service Committee 2–3)

food, as well as to give emergency relief when necessary" (35). In addition, we can insist that long-term development aid be channeled through groups working toward self-reliance for indigenous peoples.

A third step (not necessarily chronologically) is to amend our own pattern of food consumption. This means becoming aware of what goes into the process of providing food calories. For example, for every calorie of human energy that Chinese farmers spend growing and harvesting rice, they obtain 53.5 consumable calories. On the other hand, to produce one pound of beefsteak (about 1,500 calories), it takes 10,000 production calories, chiefly in the form of crops to feed livestock. This has moved a number of persons to forswear the eating of red meat, not because their personal choice will change the livestock industry, but because it is their way of identifying with the poor and negating systems that work against efficient and equitable feeding of the world.

Responsible persons are careful about their shopping habits. They do selective boycotting of agribusiness and of MNCs whose behavior in the world is particularly reprehensible. As already mentioned, some years ago the Nestlé Company was under fire for promoting the sale of infant formula in third world countries without adequate instruction in sanitary preparation and to the detriment of breast feeding which prevents a number of the sanitation problems, not to mention providing immunities for the child and acting as a natural form of birth control for the mother. Many individuals and organizations boycotted Nestlé's products (e.g. Stouffer's foods) until changes were made in their advertising of infant formula.

Del Monte is another conglomerate worth critiquing, not because of a specific action, but because of its monopolistic nature:

> [Del Monte] is the world's largest canner of fruits and vegetables. But it does more than processing and canning. It manufactures its own cans and prints its own labels; it conducts its own agricultural research; it grows produce on its own land, as well as putting 10,000 farmers under production contracts; it distributes its produce through its own banana transports, tuna seiners, air-

freight forwarding stations, ocean terminal and trucking operations; it operates its own warehouses; it maintains 58 sales offices throughout the world; and it caters 28 restaurants and provides food services to United Air Lines. (40)

Del Monte is agribusiness par excellence, manipulating produce prices, needing large quantities of cheap labor "on demand," and doing little in terms of the long-term welfare of these workers. One can avoid supporting such endeavors by joining food co-ops that buy from small farmers. (Whatever increase in price is encountered by avoiding large-scale agribusiness products can be made up by the low overhead of co-op food distribution.) One can buy directly from farmers (e.g. farmer's markets) or do his or her own personal subsistence gardening.

In terms of cooking, one can avoid overly processed foods, eat raw vegetables which saves energy, stick with simple proteins, experiment with vegetarian recipes (try the *Moosewood* and *Enchanted Broccoli Forest* cookbooks), substitute raisins and peanuts for crunchy snack foods, and guard carefully against food waste. Such practices will not immediately feed the starving children in Africa, but they will cause one to remember such children and model responsible action *vis-à-vis* the issue of malnutrition.

Shelter

Another area that needs to be addressed by those attempting to live responsibly is that of shelter. There are, of course, many housing "projects" operating in the world. One of the most sound in terms of integrating self-help with outside aid is Habitat for Humanity. In locations throughout the third world (including U.S. cities), the indigenous poor and middle-class volunteers sweat side by side to provide decent houses. This organization, and others like it, believe in empowering the poor. But the middle class itself needs to be empowered to live with integrity and wholeness.

Some persons opt for group households, sharing space and material goods, which results in less gratuitous consumerism per family. Cluster housing is a less radical option than communal living. Persons living in apartments or houses in close proximity can share common recreation areas, garden space and workshop areas. They can buy food in bulk and own appliances communally. Some groups seeking responsible living choose to live together as a basis for social action. The Philadelphia Life Center (part of the Movement for a New Society) is such a community. Eighteen Quaker families live together, lobby for peace and jobs issues, own a Land Trust Company which equalizes mortgage payments for members, and hold "clearance meetings" for personal decision making.

Work

The workplace is a constant concern for those choosing to live responsibly. Everywhere, attention needs to be paid to the provision of safe workplaces and anti-discriminatory practices. Unions have been the traditional lobby for fair hiring, safety, and wages. But in the first world unions have tended to become well-entrenched, top-heavy bureaucracies, whereas, in some places in the third world, workers can still be arrested for belonging to unions. Careful study of labor conditions in poor nations is a very important action for people of conscience, as is supporting international unions that build bridges between labor in first and third world nations. But, in addition, people in rich nations need to consider alternatives to the prosperity-motivated work ethic that so often drives us.

An interesting approach to work, shelter and lifestyle is presented by Alpha Farm in Deadwood, Oregon. The project consists of a 280 acre farm with a cafe/book-and-craft store, a hardware store, and a construction-contracting business. Most participants either farm or work in one of these small businesses. All income is shared in common and all work is organized by teams.

No doubt this seems to be a radical alternative to most of us, but there are ways that each of us can make work more meaningful and team-spirited where we are. There are ways that each of us can lobby for fairer distribution of profits for workers. Professionals ought to know how non-professionals in their organizations are hired and compensated and be willing to speak out on their behalf.

Workers need to work to keep their unions viable and representative of *all* interests. The creation of jobs should be the concern of every person working in the private or public sector. Most of all, we need to remind ourselves that work is part of what it means to be human, and dignified working conditions are the right of every person—professional, skilled technician, *campesino,* and unskilled urban dweller alike.

Health Care

Health care needs to be addressed by any responsible person. Since the U.S. is the only industrialized nation other than South Africa without a national health program, one could well claim that we have a great deal to learn from developing countries such as Nicaragua who have had to design massive health programs for basic survival. A good example of what can happen when folks ban together to supply such services, in spite of exclusive insurance systems, is project "Country Doc" in Seattle, Washington. This clinic-based program has twenty staff members, including doctors, nurse practitioners, physicians' assistants, mental health counselors, social workers, lab technicians, a pharmacist, and community health nurses. With such a staff the approach to healing and prevention can be holistic. There is an assistance fund to pay for "emergencies" which is necessary in that only 20 percent of the participants have full medical coverage. In short, the community is serving itself without waiting for federal reforms in health insurance and clinical services.

Energy

Responsible persons can live with less energy consumption. They can learn to utilize passive and active solar energy, small-scale hydroelectricity, wind, alcohol, biogas, waste heat from industry and other forms of "recyclable" energy (even something as simple as venting an electric dryer indoors during winter months). They can alter car use and save fuel. As Ivan Illich describes the attitude to car travel in rich countries:

The typical American male devotes more than 1600 hours a year to his car. He sits in it while it goes and while it stands idling. He parks it and searches for it. He earns the money to put down on it and to meet the monthly install-ments. He works to pay for petrol, tools, insurance, taxes and tickets. He spends four of his 16 waking hours on the road or gathering his resources for it. And this figure does not take into account the time consumed by other activities dictated by transport: time spent in hospitals, traffic courts and garages. . . . The model American put in 1600 hours to get 7500 miles: less than five miles per hour. In countries deprived of a transportation industry, people manage to do the same, walking wherever they want to go, and they allocate only three to eight percent of their society's time budget to traffic instead of 28 percent. What distinguishes the traffic in rich countries from the traffic in poor coun-tries is not more mileage per hour of life-time for the major-ity, but more hours of compulsory consumption of high doses of energy, packaged and unequally distributed by the transportation industry. (American Friends 206)

Lobbying for public transportation systems and car-pooling are both part of the conscientious life, as is occasionally staying home!

Case Studies

No doubt each one of us could add one or two areas of interest to the ones discussed. People sharing ideas about lifestyle with one another is what this chapter is all about. Some interesting case studies include a church in Knoxville, Tennessee that sponsors garden projects for elderly persons living in low-income housing, and the drywall worker who brings home scrap lumber intended for the trash heap to burn in his woodstove. There is the woman living in Calcutta who gave away one of her two pairs of slacks and found that the remaining pair was good for two winters. A man in Heston, Kansas put solar collectors on his home for $2,500 and received a tax credit of 55 percent. A family in Sante Fe, New Mexico uses a compost toilet to save water. One in Newton, Kansas recycles bath water as part of its farm irrigation system. And a North American family living in Zaire has discovered that simple meals co-prepared by guests is a very significant way of entertaining. (All of these examples come from *Living More with Less.*)

Why should one make all of this effort? Because the *pattern* of consumption taken for granted in rich countries perpetuates poverty through media-export of consumerism, military spending, and insensitive policies on the part of giant corporations. North Americans use five and a half times as much energy as the average world citizen and 54 times as much as a resident of India. We spend billions of dollars a year for military purposes. In Brazil foreign investment has been associated with the destruction of 40 percent of its rain forests, a cattle ranch on 140,000 acres of internal land (run by Volkswagen), and the eviction of *campesinos* from a plot of land the size of Connecticut for foreign business. Nine of the biggest U.S. banks have an average of 57 percent of their collective capital on loan to Brazil who, near bankruptcy, cannot make the interest payments. (American Friends 227–231)

Individually we are not creating the problem. *Systemic* change is necessary both in developing countries and developed countries to redistribute adequately wealth among and within nations. Yet it is individuals who start movements and they start them from a basis of commitment. What do members of a ceramic cooperative in Bolivia, St. Francis and the suburban dweller who recycles glass and aluminum have in common? A sense that human beings have too much dignity to be forever manipulated by unjust, consumer-oriented economic systems. They have the power to act and, in action, to begin their liberation from poverty and gluttony alike.

BIBLIOGRAPHY

American Friends Service Committee. *Taking Charge of Our Lives: Living Responsibly in the World,* edited by Joan Bodner. San Francisco: Harper and Row, 1981.

Boff, Leonardo. *Saint Francis: A Model for Human Liberation,* translated by John Diercksmeier. New York: Crossroad, 1984.

Freire, Paulo. *Pedagogy of the Oppressed,* translated by Myra Ramos. New York: Continuum, 1983.

Goulet, Denis. "Development as Liberation: Policy Lessons from Case Studies," *World Development* 7:555–566 (1979).

de Kadt, Emanuel. "Community Participation for Health: The Case of Latin America," *World Development* 10:573–584 (1982).

Longacre, Doris Jansen. *Living More with Less*. Scottdale, Pennsylvania: Herald Press (1980).

Suggestions for Further Study

American Friends Service Committee. *Taking Charge of Our Lives: Living Responsibly in the World,* edited by Joan Bodner. San Francisco: Harper and Row, 1981.

Freire, Paulo, translated by Myra Ramos. *Pedagogy of the Oppressed*. New York: Continuum, 1983.

Longacre, Doris Jansen. *Living More With Less*. Scottdale, Pennsylvania: Herald Press, 1980.

Mother Earth News, any collection of issues.

Books for consultation, rather than study, include:
Lappe, Frances M. *Diet for a Small Planet*. New York: Ballantine, 1982.

Longacre, Doris Jansen. *The More With Less Cookbook*. Scottdale, Pennsylvania: Herald Press, 1976.

Discussion Questions and Activities

1. Start with some storytelling. Each of you should recount your greatest victory over fear and impotence. What originally convinced you that you could not do what you wanted to do? What finally gave you the power to do it? Can you relate these feelings to the plight of the poor who feel trapped in their situations?

2. In the last month, what things have you collectively purchased that you did not need. Make a list on newsprint. Then go down the list and speculate about what prompted the purchases. Discuss ways that you can take more charge of your buying.

3. Each of you take a few moments to jot down everything that you can remember eating in the last twenty-four hours. In terms of basic nutrition, chemical additives, and packaging, how far away are these items from the original food source? Does it strike you as odd that in the first world people pay more to eat less calories because overweight and obsession with appearances are rampant? (What do you think a third world community would think about our epidemic of bulimia?) How can you be more conscientious about food shopping and preparation?

4. How many unnecessary car trips did each of you take this week? Could some of them have been avoided by walking? It might be interesting to covenant with one another to cut back automobile use by 10 percent or even 30 percent for a week. Keep a list of ways that you "manage" to do without during the week. Then bring the lists with you the next time that you get together and decide which coping mechanisms were most successful and therefore might become permanent parts of your lifestyles.

5. Read quickly over your response journals and bring up issues that appear there.

Building a Basic Needs Community

Community is a word that gets bandied about in our society almost to the point of being devoid of meaning. Perhaps the reason we talk of it so often and strain to apply it where it hardly fits is because we experience so little real community. In *Habits of the Heart,* a recent non-fiction best seller, Robert Bellah and his associates explore the loss of community in North American culture for the sake of our famed "rugged individualism." We prize individualism in therapy, in business ventures, in education, in our families, in churches, and even in philanthropy (think of all those donor plaques).

There is no doubt that self-actualization and individuation are important concepts for our age. They are important to us, not only because we live in the post-Freudian century, not only because of the "American dream," but also because these concepts have *always* been operative in human development to some extent. Yet, the need to come together in cooperative groups, and to reflect on the nature of those groups, has been equally constant in human history.

Western culture begins, in part, with the development of the Greek *polis.* The word originally meant "citadel" or the whole people that used the citadel. It came to refer to the "common cultural life" shared by these people. Religion, art, games, and the discussion of important ideas could only reach fulfillment in Greek society through the *polis.* Plato gave universal credibility to the idea of the *polis* through his description of the perfect society, the Republic. Still, we also remember the Greeks as champions of the individual.

The trick for any society is to maintain a balance between human needs for the flourishing of the individual and for the stability/integrity of community. These needs ought to be balanced in almost every endeavor we undertake, including our commitment to the world's poor. The title and preface to this book clearly state the notion that personal and global needs must be integrated. Chapter One explores the global dimensions of personal moral development. Chapter Two examines community on both a tribal and universal level and concludes that group consciousness itself must be expansive, lest the group become ingrown and insular. The discussion questions at the end of each chapter try to bring the readers' consciousness of global issues down to the day-to-day level of immediate relationships and personal conduct.

This chapter will attempt to keep the balance between centripetal (inward) and centrifugal (outward) consciousness alive. It will also examine local communities as both efficient and satisfying means to accomplish the long-term task of global involvement, and as a models of interdependence and mutual respect which the global order needs so badly.

In terms of the "efficiency" of communal action, the *Handbook* for Amnesty International states, "When a dozen people pool their resources of commitment, creativity, and perseverance, they discover a power worth much more than the sum of its parts." Yet it also goes on to describe the *expanded* community that develops between "doers" and "recipients." For instance, the base Christian communities which have taken shape in Latin America in recent decades initially arose out of specific, local pastoral needs but have come to see themselves as attempts to model the kingdom of God which is not yet fully present.

What we are proposing in this chapter is that people interested in global issues form small groups or cell groups of persons willing to study the issues further and to design action in response to that study, and that these same groups undertake specific development projects as they work to model the kind of cooperative behavior that they crave for world society. The cooperative interdependence of nations, like the kingdom of God, is an unrealized dream, but it has no chance at all without careful reflection on the problems, work on specific areas of concern, and a vision for change that can be implemented on some level, no matter how small or seemingly insignificant. We will begin by looking at definitions of community. Then we will look at three different models of community: the kibbutz, the university, and base Christian communities. Finally, we will examine how global interests have been and can be channeled through communities of commitment.

Definitions of Community

Martin Buber, who has written a great deal about the relationship of person to person, defines community as "the being no longer side by side but *with* one another of a multitude of persons" (31). Bonhoeffer defines it in terms of Christian development, claiming that a purely spiritual life is both dangerous and abnormal, in that "God has willed that we should seek and find His living Word in the witness of a brother" (23). Community is the context for God's revelation in Bonhoeffer's theology.

Maurice Friedman claims that the truest element of community is tension. Community may be a protection against isolation and a celebration of togetherness, but it should never smother otherness. What he seeks is a practice of togetherness that preserves each member's self-actualization. Toward this end he distinguishes the community of affinity ("always ultimately false community") from the community of otherness ("a way of being faithful and diverse at the same time") (136). He applies this distinction particularly to the learning community. A learning community that channels conflict into dialogue rather than forcing it into false harmony is a genuine community. This kind of dialogue requires careful hearing because it does not stem from linguistic homogeneity, the participants recognizing that truth is never something we *have,* it is something we relate to.

One of the most recent and widely read explorations of community is *The Different Drum: Community-Making and Peace* by M. Scott Peck. In the beginning of his study, Peck makes the bold claim that "in and through community lies the salvation of the world" (17). Obviously he is not talking about any particular community, but the dynamic by which communities come together. He recognizes the equal pulls of *individuation* and *interdependence* in human personality, and, with that in mind, defines community as "a group of individuals who have learned how to communicate honestly with each other, whose relationships go deeper than the masks of composure, and who have developed some significant commitment to 'rejoice together, mourn together,' and to 'delight in each other, make others' conditions our own' " (59). His conditions for community include that it be *inclusive,* allowing for individual differences, that it be *realistic, contemplative, safe,* and *a laboratory for personal disarmament.* A true community knows how to fight gracefully, draws knowledge and energy from conflict, and consists of all leaders, sharing leadership.

How does it come into being? Often a community develops in response to crisis (Alcoholics Anonymous is a perfect example), but it can happen by chance or design. Usually it passes through four stages: *pseudocommunity,* where conflict is avoided and superficial likenesses are celebrated; *chaos,* where honest struggle becomes vital; *emptiness,* where members give up a number of their expectations, prejudices, missionary zeal, and need for control; and finally *community,* where real healing and conversion can take place because they are not forced.

Having established what true community is, Scott Peck goes on to comment that in spite of our recent fascination for how community functions, we make no effort to conduct ourselves as world citizens as if any of it made sense. In fact "it seems that the rules by which nations behave are generally antithetical to virtually everything we know about the rules of community-making" (165). His solution would be to start with the integrity of the smaller community, then to work by modeling and analogy to the larger whole. For example, he takes a look at U.S. foreign policy. It is a premise of AA that the only person you can change is yourself; but our political and spiritual leadership concludes that America's role is to change other countries through manipulation. If we tried to make ourselves the best possible society, to concentrate on the integrity of our internal relationships, might we not become a proactive example of respectful cooperation?

This is not to say that indigenous communities should become isolationist and in-grown (tribalistic), but that only through practicing honest analysis and dialogic tolerance *internally* can groups truly learn how to transcend their specific culture and "worry about the whole world." Scott Peck's perception is that nations often refuse to go through the necessary "emptiness" of admitting that they have been wrong, and so cannot grow into world community. Small communities of peace-makers, careful of their procedures, respectful of their members, and unwilling to be either isolationists or manipulators, can, in fact, so merge task and method that they become prophetic practitioners of peace.

This is a fairly hopeful view. Glenn Tinder in his *Community: Reflections on a Tragic Ideal* is more tenuous. He looks to "the perfect harmony of whole and part" proposed by Plato and Rousseau and sees that it reflects only half of the human condition. It is an imperative of human nature to live in community, but time, space, and death legislate against true, lasting integration of will with will. We live with others in history, but constantly seek our individual selfhood. Therefore, "man is a communal being who, in his finitude, mortality, and pride, enters only fragmentary and ephemeral communities" (177).

Ephemeral or permanent, the existence of communities in history is a constant. Taking a look at three widespread practices of community can help us to explore both the universal and temporary elements of this phenomenon.

Models of Community

The Kibbutz

The kibbutz is a form of communal life and work that began in Palestine around the turn of the century, gained momentum during the 1930's, and still exists today. It arose partially out of the crisis of anti-semitic persecution in Europe that culminated in the holocaust. European Jews, seeking freedom and safety, emigrated to Palestine to live and work in self-sufficient, protected, agrarian communities. But the development of lifestyle in these communities was equally reflective of members' reactions against life in the *stetl*. In Jewish communities in Europe, life was hierarchical and unegalitarian. Religion was an overintellectualized phenomenon, and concentration on personal piety separated the adherents from social and economic problems. The kibbutz became "a purposeful attempt to learn and develop more just ways of achieving the quality of life" (Blasi 4). A final cause for its formation was

Zionism—the desire of the Jews to achieve a distinctive political identity and to become a self-determined people. As of 1980 there were some 240 kibbutzim in existence, housing approximately 94,000 people (3.3 percent of the population of Israel) (4).

One of the key values that determines life in the kibbutz is the moral value of physical labor. Work is a human need, a creative act that has ultimate value. It is the way to become one with self, society and nature. Therefore, all work on the kibbutz is performed by live-in members; no tasks are hired out. Property used by the community and goods produced by its members belong to the entire community, thereby avoiding the evils of land speculation, absentee ownership, unearned income from rent, and the disruptive split between gentry and peasantry. All work is rewarded equally, but need takes precedence over equality when medical care or special diets are required. There is no censorship of reading material or speech, but behavior is expected to be characterized by mutual aid or welfare. Likewise, town meetings are often the scenes of vigorous debate, where individual views are passionately defended. But once a decision is made, members are expected to respect them as resulting from collective wisdom.

Kiryat Yedidim is a representative example. It was founded in the 1930's, primarily by Polish immigrants. In the mid-1950's it had 500 members, 250 of them children. The communal dining hall is the physical and social center of the community; houses (each a room and a half, with porch and bathroom) run in parallel rows on either side. A communal laundry, sewing room, clothing storehouse, library, reading room, and school complete the inner buldings. On the periphery are sheds, barns, carpentry shops, warehouses, etc. Work projects include dairy farming, cultivation of field crops, vegetable gardens, fishing, fruit orchards, poultry raising, and production of fodder. Productive work (that which produces income) absorbs about 50 percent of the daily work hours; non-productive work (maintenance of the community) absorbs the other 50 percent. Jobs are primarily assigned by choice; unpleasant tasks are assigned by rotation.

Life in *Kiryat Yedidim* promotes the equality of men and women. Women are the total economic equals of men, and they are not bound by traditional marriage. Couples join by asking to share a room, and the kibbutz accepts the economic and practical responsibility for raising children, who live together with nurses and teachers, visiting their parents in the late afternoon and on holidays.

Intellectual and artistic endeavors are encouraged, although not at the expense of physical labor. They are integrated into day-to-day work responsibilities rather than being isolated as distinct vocations. No artists or scholars are economically compensated for their efforts.

Politically the kibbutz has assumed a prophetic role—it is intentionally a model for a new society based on collective living (a "socialist island in the middle of a sea of capitalism"). Therefore it experiences tension with Israel's "reformist" government and with its increasingly materialistic populace.

Where are the problems at *Kiryat Yedidim?* A number of them stem from the discontent of women. True, women have been emancipated from the domestic subservience of traditional marriage, but thay have proved unable to perform some of the more strenuous farming tasks in the kibbutz and so have generally been assigned to maintenance jobs. This puts them back into traditional "female" tasks, but without the satisfaction of taking pride in their own homes. They resent seeing their children only at prescribed hours and worry about aging in a culture where marriages are not protected by law. Both men and women get tired of the crowded, noisy dining room, and of the indignities of public showers. (The influx of visitors and work crews wanting to "experience kibbutz life" has not helped these complaints.) Furthermore, as Israel has taken its place in world diplomatic and economic systems and become more cosmopolitan, the ideals of the kibbutz seem to be outside rather than exemplary of the ideals of the state.

Kibbutzim are providing for more privacy of families and are allowing a higher standard of living these days. But more people are leaving the communities than in the days of austerity. Some argue that the crisis which caused them has passed, others that their work of reformation has barely begun. How they transform themselves to meet new demands from inside and out will be interesting to watch.

The University

Paul Goodman laments that the present university is not what it ought to be, not what it was designed to be—a genuine community of scholars. While it remains "the only important face-to-face self-governing community still active in our modern society," it has sold out to the corporate model. While it remains a small city with a heterogeneous population, it has gone from bottom-up governance, to top-down coordination. It has all but given up its struggle with the world, and mistakes failure to act for harmony of interests.

To make his point, he goes back to the student covenant at the early University of Bologna. Students swore "fraternal charity, mutual association and amity, the consolation of the sick and support of the needy, the conduct of funerals and the extirpation of rancor and quarrels, the attendance and escort of one's *doctorandi* to and from the place of examination; and the spiritual advantage of members" (18). In short, students designed themselves into a community concerned for the total welfare of its members. It was "an intramural city with a universal culture," a place where intellectual debate was encouraged as a prelude to the community's "electric clash" with the surrounding culture. The emphasis was on the relationship between students, and between students and faculty, that is, on the pursuit of subject matter *with* someone or on teaching it *for* someone.

In the present climate, he argues, the community of scholars has been burdened with "pomp and size that are irrelevant to education" (61). Top-heavy administrative structures make it "hardly distinguishable from the extramural world." Buildings are refined show pieces; boards of trustees demand multiple ground-breakings and other meaningless ceremonies. Curriculum is standardized for efficiency and to meet state requirements. Class size is increased to make learning more lucrative. Students are encouraged to think about abstract issues but ignore the hard task of practicing democracy on campus. In short, institutions of higher education have become orderly, efficient, homogeneous degree factories, maintaining only the vestiges of a true community.

Could the university reclaim some of its grassroots viability? Goodman argues yes, and encourages schools to experiment with their structures and modes of governance. In terms of size, schools should be kept small, and universities should be divided into schools. Each school should be "small enough for face-to-face relations, to insure frequent meetings of students and the collegiate teachers, and conversation and commensalism of students with the same studies"; at the same time, each should be "large enough to have a well-rounded assortment of teachers and students" (133). The medieval university was under 500, which might be a rule of thumb.

Goodman feels that a majority of teachers should be veterans of the world—professionals who teach rather than professional teachers. That is, teachers should be vitally connected with the world, either through vocation or interest. They should also be able and willing to withdraw from the world for critical evaluation. This critical evaluation, carried on in the presence of students and in dialogue with students, should move toward the ideal, for only when they possess ideals do students have the vision to transform practice as they enter the world at large.

Likewise, students should be encouraged to evaluate their communal environment critically, to spot malpractice and to argue for its eradication, even if that makes the governance of the institution more cumbersome. Chaos is the crucible out of which new ideas arise. Students should be more responsible for their own living arrangements and have less things ready-made for them, including the curriculum.

Ideally the role of curriculum is not to plan for society but to outgrow it. Courses of study which do not appear to be practical one year may supply ample jobs the next. And some courses of study may never lead to specific jobs, but to the creative performance of many jobs. (English majors are finally realizing this, but only because some clever CEOs discovered that articulate, well-read executives wear well. The real task will have been accomplished when humanities and business majors transform the corporation into a more humane, democratic structure because they have learned the value of difference.)

One of the reasons Goodman feels that a restoration of the community of scholars is possible is that it has never totally ceased to exist. Just read the promotional material of any institution of higher education. The values it promotes are the ones that have always kept alive the idea of the university as a crucible of society, a place where students and faculty can wrestle with the idea of community and where they can prepare to call the culture at large into question.

Base Christian Communities

In Latin America small groups of Christians, committed to Bible study, group welfare, and the reformation of social structures, are replacing the parish as the primary unit of Catholicism. In Brazil alone there are more than 70,000 of these communities, with a total membership of over two and a half million (Berryman 63). These groups arise out of a specific pastoral problem—parishes in rural areas and urban shantytowns often have only one priest for 20,000 persons. To rely on centralized church leadership means that many spiritual needs of the people simply go unheeded. Decentralized associations of believers are able to fill the gap.

There are several antecedents to the base Christian community. In the early twentieth century a young Belgian priest, Joseph Cardign, became interested in reaching the working classes. He held small group meetings of young factory workers which stressed taking action toward the solution of people's problems. Their procedure was to observe a problem, judge it, and then act. At the next meeting they would evaluate the outcome of the action. This developed into the Young Christian Workers and the Christian Family Movement, both of which came to Latin America in the 1950's. The church renewal movements in Spain, with their weekend retreats, were also influential on the development of small Christian communities.

In the late 1950's there was a movement in Latin America to train catechists who could celebrate services in place of a priest. Then in their First Nationwide Pastoral Plan (1965–70), the Brazilian bishops called for a subdivision of parishes into "basic communities." At the same time a group of priests from Chicago began experimental pastoral work outside of Panama City. Their adult dialogue groups became so effective that they were visited by many and their methods copied and adapted. When the Catholic bishops met in Medellín in 1968, the base communities received strong affirmation and further definition: "It is the first and fundamental ecclesiastical nucleus, which down on the grass-roots level brings richness and expansion to the faith—and to religious worship, which is its expression. This community, which is the initial cell of the Church and the radiating center for its evangelizing efforts, is today a most potent factor for human advancement and development" (Marins 1).

Generally the communities exist in rural areas or on the fringes of the city. They are run by lay people, with a priest's help. They arise primarily among the poor and around celebration of the word, prayer and mutual help. They often move toward socio-political study and action. They have replaced the anonymous large parishes with communities of commitment, personal growth, dialogue and critical thinking. As Harvey Cox describes them, they present "a new type of community which places the person within a skein of relationships that is neither an archaic tribal form nor a continuation of modern individualism" (127). He goes on to say that these communities have established a sense of *polis* where it has never existed or where it has been destroyed by political repression.

The truth of that last statement has caused trouble for some of the base Christian communities in Latin America, because the empowerment of the poor, which is a logical outcome of their beginning to study and act on their problems, does not sit well with highly centralized, elitist governments. In Paraguay, a community of peasants from Jequi decided to unify their work, efforts at self-education, and practice of faith. Toward this end they moved together to the wilderness, bought land, and built a community which was so successful that it became a model for other peasant communities. Because common reflection and prayer in these communities often led to common work, common purchases, and common sales of agricultural products, they were accused of being communists and attacked by government troops, spurred on by nervous landowners.

This kind of government response has occurred in El Salvador and other places. The pressure on these communities not to exist is strong, and some dissolve. But many persevere, because, as Cox explains, the "religious ethos of the base communities proclaims that the meaning of human life is to be found in the struggle for God's reign" (130). Like the kibbutz and the true community of scholars, the base Christian community gains its energy not just from the collective but from its prophetic role in society.

Communities of Commitment

The communities here described are total ones—they involve where people live, the work they do, their emerging ideologies, and the actions that they take. As such, they emphasize in an intense fashion the dynamics of successful community—heterogeneity, decentralized leadership, the ability to deal with conflict, mutual commitment. They also illustrate, in a dramatic fashion, the problems faced by many communities—disillusionment, pressure from outside forces, the ever-present assertion of personal interests, false ideals of harmony.

But not all communities are this pervasive. There are groups of people who come together for a weekend and feel themselves to be in community. There are groups who meet once a week, or even once a month, to accomplish limited goals, who are real communities. It is this type of gathering that may well arise out of your commitment to global issues.

There are a number of groups operating in our society with the dual goals of understanding social problems and taking action toward their alleviation. The authors of *Pedagogy for the Non-Poor* stress the fact that most persons wanting to engage in social action need a community of support to be able to do so. The group provides them with dialogic reflection on issues, with a vehicle for social analysis, with a call to realism, and with accountability. It also provides them with moral support in the accomplishment of difficult tasks.

Groups that work this way include Amnesty International (discussed more extensively in Chapter Seven). The working groups of Amnesty, the ones who actually contact and "serve" specific political prisoners, meet once or twice a month and call themselves communities. Their meetings involve fellowship, education, and action. In addition, groups reach out to the larger community through articles, speaking engagements, posters, etc. They try to do the kind of supportive networking among themselves that they intentionally do with prisoners and their families.

The Parenting for Peace and Justice Network supports small groups of families who want information and opportunities for action. Families support one another through job and personal problems, but also combine to deal with social issues. They might adopt a third world community, join demonstrations for common causes, or undertake letter-writing projects. It is their way of taking the family seriously without deifying the nuclear family and without ignoring the larger human family.

The Plant Closures Project focuses on a particular social problem. Task forces in this project engage in direct action, legislative lobbying, economic development for the victims of closures, and support for the effects of closures—alcoholism, drug abuse, wife and child abuse, etc. Their membership crosses racial and ethnic lines and is as willing to discuss personal problems as economic factors and political strategies.

An interesting example of the short-term, intense community experience is provided by Traveling for Transformation. Recognizing the need for face-to-face encounter with human need, and for community support and accountability in the work to alleviate human need, they plan three week immersion seminars which concentrate on the systemic social, economic and political problems manifest in relations between the first and third worlds. They concentrate on regional groups, encourage journal keeping, and suggest the formation of covenant partners to keep commitment alive.

The list could continue, but that would not solve the problem of what you are going to do about all of this. Chances are you are reading this book with a group of like-minded, but not identical people. Chances are you are reading it together because you are moving toward or are already engaged in some kind of basic needs work. You may already have a kind of community or be working toward one. Hopefully, the material in this chapter has helped you to see your group more clearly and critically, to assess what its importance is to you and to the larger communities in which you exist.

There is no formula for community; each group must set its

own parameters in terms of meeting times, procedures, what to do in times of crisis, how to maintain commitment, etc. What we would suggest is that you keep in mind the need for certain polarities and the need to work toward their integration. Study and action must exist together. If you wait to understand a situation in order to act on it, you'll most likely never get there. If you act without analysis, your action can be misguided and abortive. Conflict and consensus must play equal roles in your dialogue. Do not pretend to agree for the "sake of harmony." Learn to express alternate points of view and to listen to them, not insisting that a particular jargon be used. But when an action has been chosen by the group, do not spend all of your time dissenting and second guessing the decision.

The microcosm and the macrososm both deserve your attention. Your immediate community and the world community both demand justice and care. A person who can love and serve his or her family, but never thinks about Nelson Mandela rotting in prison in South Africa, does not really understand community. Nor does the person who can love and serve the orphans of El Salvador but not say a civil thing to Aunt Alice. The two planes are intimately connected, which is why, in the area of global justice, the end never justifies the means. Communities of commitment serve the larger community by the actions they take, by the ways in which they model honest interdependence, and by the context they provide for personal integrity.

We encourage you to find a course of study for your group— perhaps a specific global problem, such as population control, or a troubled area of the world. Increase what you presently know about world poverty so that you continually preserve the integrity of the complexity of the problem. We also encourage you to find a way of acting on your convictions about what you are learning—to consider visiting the third world for purposes of work or accompanying the poor on their journey, to consider funding a particular basic needs project, to consider becoming a sister community to a third world village or settlement, to consider taking some of the political actions listed in Chapter Eight, to consider educating others through informal presentations of your experiences. (Agencies that can help you arrange some of these activities are listed in

"Suggestions for Further Study" at the end of the chapter.) We encourage you to spend time together discussing personal issues and misgivings you have about what you are attempting to accomplish. Most of all, we encourage you to laugh at yourselves when you become pompous, overexacting, and otherwise excessively first world in your attempts to solve rather than participate in the solution of third world problems. You will do all of these things, and more. A speculative community is free to make mistakes, and to enjoy themselves, and to cry over the terrible injustices that exist in spite of all of their efforts. And they are free to change the rules. Who knows but that such compassionate flexibility might someday define the international scene—well, part of it.

Bibliography

Amnesty International USA: Group Members' Handbook. New York: Amnesty International USA, 1985.

Basic Christian Communities. Washington D.C.: Latin American Documentation, 1976.

Berryman, Phillip. *Liberation Theology.* New York: Pantheon Books, 1987.

Blasi, Joseph Raphael. *The Communal Future: the Kibbutz and the Utopian Dilemma.* Norwood, PA: Norwood Editions, 1980.

Bonhoeffer, Dietrich. *Life Together,* translated by John D. Doberstein. New York: Harper and Brothers, 1954.

Buber, Martin. *Between Man and Man,* translated by Ronald Gregor Smith. Boston: Beacon Press, 1955.

The Concept of Community: Readings with Interpretation, edited by David W. Minar and Scott Greer. Chicago: Aldine Publishing Company, 1969.

Cox, Harvey. *Religion in the Secular City: Toward a Post-Modern Theology.* New York: Simon and Schuster, 1984.

Evans, Alice Frazer, et al. *Pedagogies for the Non-Poor.* Maryknoll, New York: Orbis Books, 1987.

Fishman, Aryei. *The Religious Kibbutz Movement: The Revival of the Jewish Religious Community.* Jerusalem: Jerusalem Post Press, 1957.

Friedman, Maurice. *The Confirmation of Otherness*. New York: The Pilgrim Press, 1983.

Gerlach, Luther P. and Virginia Hines. *People, Power, Change: Movements of Social Transformation*. Indianapolis: Bobbs-Merrill Educational Publishing, 1970.

Manins, José. "Basic Christian Communities in Latin America," *Basic Christian Communities* (Latin American Documentation). Washington D.C., 1976.

Peck, M. Scott. *The Different Drum: Community-Making and Peace*. New York: Simon and Schuster, 1987.

Spiro, Melford E. *Kibbutz: Venture in Utopia*. Cambridge: Harvard University Press, 1956.

Tinder, Glenn. *Community: Reflections on a Tragic Ideal*. Baton Rouge: Louisiana State University Press, 1980.

SUGGESTIONS FOR FURTHER STUDY

Adler, Ronald B. and Neil Towne. *Looking Out—Looking In*. New York: H. Holt and Company, 1984.

Evans. Alice et al. *Pedagogies for the Non-Poor*. Maryknoll: Orbis Books, 1987.

Galdamez, Pablo. *Faith of a People: The Life of a Basic Christian Community in El Salvador*, translated by Robert R. Barr. Maryknoll, New York: Orbis Books, 1986.

Peck, M. Scott. *The Different Drum: Community-Making and Peace*. New York: Simon and Schuster, 1987.

Agencies that facilitate development education include:
Basic Needs International (Box 36, Wayne, Pennsylvania 19087).
The Hunger Project (Global Office, 1 Madison Aenue, New York, New York 10010).
Society for International Development (Palazzo Civita del Lavoro, 00144 Rome, Italy).

Agencies that arrange third world study and/or work tours include:
The Center for Global Education (713 21st Ave., S. Minneapolis, Minnesota 55424).
Food First (145 Ninth St., San Francisco, California, 94193).

Global Awareness Through Experience/G.A.T.E. (Box 3042, Harlingen, Texas 78551).
Our Developing World (13004 Paseo Presada, Saratoga, California 95070).
Plowshares Institute (Box 243, Simsbury, Connecticut 06070).

Agencies that can help you select and support a basic needs project in a third world country (or in a third world section of the first world) include:
Any of the agencies listed, with addresses, in Chapter Seven.
Graduate schools that have programs in economic development, and whose students are required to do field work.
Denominational offices for international and inner-city ministries.

Agencies that can help you support job creation projects within a third world community include:
Action International/AITEC (10-C Mount Auburn St., Cambridge, Massachusetts 02138).
Opportunity International (P.O. Box 3695, Oak Brook, IL 60522).

Two agencies that can keep you abreast of current legislative actions impinging on world justice and hunger are:
Bread for the World (802 Rhode Island Ave., N.E., Washington, D.C. 20018).
IMPACT (100 Maryland Avenue, N.E., Washington, D.C. 20002).

DISCUSSION QUESTIONS AND ACTIVITIES

1. Of the three models of community discussed at length—the kibbutz, the university, and the base Christian community— which one would you be most likely to join and why? Think about this question individually (you might try to write about it in your journal), then share your responses.

2. What is the smallest community to which you belong? By what principles does it operate? How would you like to see it altered? (Again, you may want to pursue this question in your journals, then share responses.)

3. What happens to you when conflict occurs in one of your primary groups? Are you usually a participant in the debate, or a reconciler? How would you assess your participation? If you are a participant, are you making points or willing to have your position refined by the opposition? If you are a reconciler do you seek peace at any price, or a full dialogic process? Would you like to change your participation? How?

4. What kind of community do you want to see emerge within this group? How often do you think the group should meet? How should meetings be structured? How inclusive should it be? What kind of commitment do you want the members to have? What kind of actions should it pursue?

5. As a group, design a hypothetical United Nations. How would its general assembly operate? Who would lead? How would debate be handled? How would cultural exchange be integrated into business? What kind of programs would it foster?

6. Read over your response journals and discuss troublesome or interesting entries.